MANAGING DEFENSE:
JAPAN'S DILEMMA

HARRISON M. HOLLAND

UNIVERSITY
PRESS OF
AMERICA

Lanham • New York • London

Library of Congress Cataloging-in-Publication Data

Holland, Harrison M., 1921–
Managing defense : Japan's dilemma / by Harrison M. Holland.
p.   cm. Bibliography: p. Includes index.
1. Japan—Defenses. 2. Japan—Military policy. 3. Japan—Military relations—
United States. 4.   United States—Military relations—Japan. I. Title.
UA845.H584 1988   355'.033052—dc19   87–29530 CIP
ISBN 0–8191–6766–5 (alk. paper)
ISBN 0–8191–6767–3 (pbk. : alk. paper)

All University Press of America books are produced on acid-free
paper which exceeds the minimum standards set by the National
Historical Publications and Records Commission.

CONTENTS

CHAPTERS

APPENDICES

TABLES, FIGURES and MAPS

Tables

Figures

Maps

PREFACE
and
ACKNOWLEDGMENTS

Managing Defense-Japan's Dilemma, a sequel to my 1984 book, Managing Diplomacy: The United States and Japan, has a narrower focus, concentrating on the role of the bureaucrat and politician in Japanese security management. For purposes of this study, a general definition of defense management would involve the identity of those bureaucrats and politicians responsible for defense policy, the major elements in that policy and how policy decisions are made.

The defense budget, a critical factor in developing defense policy, will be used to illustrate how the bureaucrat and politician interact in dealing with the major problem facing defense policymakers - the dilemma of how to reconcile the conflicting pressures from inside and outside Japan on Japanese security management.

For the past decade, Japan's defense policy has had essentially two faces, one for the Japanese public and the other for the United States. For the Japanese public, nervous over military spending and a resurgence of militarism, government defense policies are carefully crafted to assuage such fears.

For the United States, growing increasingly impatient over the slow growth in Japanese defense capabilities and struggling with a huge defense budget, the government gives continual assurances of its intention to buildup the Self Defense forces and to assume responsibility for air and sea surveillance up to 1000 miles from Japan.

This dichotomy in defense policy has caused considerable misunderstanding between the two allies and has led to the present research.

The United States and Japan view the world differently. For the Reagan Administration, the communist threat, particularly from the Soviet Union, is the principal cause of global unrest and instability and the great challenge to freedom and democracy. The way to meet the challenge is by building economic and military strength.

Japan, while acknowledging the danger posed by Russian military adventurism, is not convinced that Japan's security is menaced by the USSR. Moreover, Japan's commitment to peaceful co-existence with her neighbors (Article 9 of the Japanese Constitution renounces war as an instrument of national policy), the deep pacifist strains in Japanese society, the public's profound suspicion of resurgent militarism, and a national commitment to economic growth and a better life for the Japanese people, have all militated against dependence on military force to achieve national goals. The result has been to downplay the military establishment, emphasize the self defense character of the army, navy, and airforce, impose a ceiling on defense spending, and equivocate when replying to U.S. urgings for a speedup in her defense effort.

It is not altogether surprising that Japan and the United States have differing outlooks on security. Japan experienced total military defeat and occupation by foreign military forces for the first time in her history, convincing her to seek influence and gain international stature through other than military means.

The United States, leading the Free World's challenge to communism and drawing heavily on her own resources to build Western defenses, grows increasingly impatient with her allies, especially Japan, for not devoting more energy and wherewithal to security.

The onus lies especially heavy on Japan because of her enormous economic power. Her unwillingness to spend more than 1% of her Gross National Product (GNP) on defense, despite her economic and financial muscle, has provoked a negative reaction in Washington. The disparity between the two allies is striking - an approximately $300 billion defense budget for the United States in FY 1987 and a $17 billion outlay for Japan in 1987. This fact alone has forced Japan to adopt ambivalent policies when dealing with the controversial defense issue at home and with U.S. insistence on a greater Japanese defense effort.

Japan presses to be treated as an equal partner, yet for political, economic and cultural reasons, which will be discussed later, she has seen fit to make only a limited contribution to her own security. The United States has often been unsympathetic to Japanese explanations.

Yet, the Japanese might be forgiven for wondering why, in light of American criticism of the uneven nature of defense responsibilities, the United States signed the U.S.-Japan Security Treaty in 1952 and the revised Treaty in 1960 which provided for the United States to come to the defense of Japan in case of attack but placed no similar obligation on Japan. The defense relationship has lacked reciprocal commitments for over 3 decades, but it has only been relatively recently that attention has been drawn to the lop-sided character of the Treaty and to the lack of equity in defense burden sharing.

Officials in the Reagan Administration and influential Congressmen and Senators have decried these circumstances and accused Japan of shirking her security responsibilities and getting a "Free Ride" at U.S. expense. This U.S. attitude has made Japanese leaders nervous, angry, and also uncertain about how to react to American criticism. To maintain a satisfactory security relationship with the United States while at the same time keeping the controversial defense issue politically manageable at home, has required the Japanese government to reassure a skeptical public that Japan's defense program will be moderate (most opinion polls reflect little or no public support for an accelerated defense buildup), and that the government would adhere to an approximately 1% ceiling on defense spending.

The government has also had to convince the United States that it is doing all that it can to meet its defense obligations. Confronted by a doubting Pentagon, an alert Japanese media, and aggressive opposition political parties, the government has had little maneuvering room. By posturing on the defense budget and on the National Defense Program Outline-NDPO-(*taiko*), Japan's defense charter since 1976, and the Mid-Term Planning Estimate-MTPE-(*chugyo*), an annual review of defense policy by the Japan Defense Agency, the government has had some success in keeping the security debate from getting out of hand.

American complaints have brought Japan face-to-face with the reality of her defense relationship with the United States - she must sooner or later allocate more money for the defense buildup program and make a greater effort to shoulder more of the general defense burden.

It is a hard decision and will require more political and budgetary dexterity than has sometimes been shown in the past. The need to articulate a defense policy acceptable to the Japanese public and to the United States has been deeply troublesome to defense planners, placing limits on their efforts to build a credible military force. If they do to little, the United States complains; if they appear to move too fast, the security debate heats up at home. Working within such narrow parameters has made managing defense more difficult.

How Japan's defense policymakers are behaving under such conditions and how defense decisions are made under these extraordinary circumstances, will be among the important questions addressed in the chapters that follow.

For the United States, in the ongoing struggle with the Soviet Union, no alliance is of greater importance than the one with Japan, despite differences over defense policy. Peace, stability and economic opportunity in the Pacific Basin depend on the determination and skill of the United States and Japan to maintain a viable and cooperative defense relationship.

The responsibility rests especially heavy on Japan and the task is not an easy one. Growing Soviet military power in Northeast Asia has severely tested the alliance. Cracks have already appeared, as I mentioned earlier, over the issue of more equitable defense burden sharing. Some in the United States are even linking the growing trade problem with the defense issue and this is leading to further misunderstandings and harsh rhetoric.

Editorial comments in Japanese newspapers and public comments by unhappy officials and politicians, for example, question the reliability of the American commitment to defend Japan under the U.S.-Japan Security Treaty. The American side replies by chiding Japan for not devoting more of its resourcces to strengthen the Self Defense Forces and for not carrying out the commitments given to President Ronald Reagan to be responsible for air and sea surveillance extending 1000 miles from the Japanese islands. This kind of mutual faultfinding undermines trust and gives comfort to adversaries of Japan and the United States.

The alliance could be strengthened, differences in perceptions better understood, and cooperation on defense policy greatly enhanced if both sides were to recognize the importance of closer and more effective consultation.

In talking with many Japanese concerned with the defense problem, I believe there are things to be done that have not yet been thoroughly tried that could improve communication and understanding and lead to a more viable partnership. I think it important, therefore, to offer my recommendations on ways to improve the defense relationship at the beginning rather than at the end of this study so the reader can note the direction I believe the relationship must go as Japan and the United States approach the last decade of the 20th century.

First, however, I want to make the following important assumptions affecting U.S.-Japan defense policy.

Assumption 1. The Japanese government will continue to spend conservatively on defense.

Assumption 2. The new 5-year defense plan, adopted as a national policy in September 1985, will afford greater flexibility to defense planners but will have only a marginal impact on defense spending. Its lack of a conceptual framework will be a handicap in developing defense policies.

Assumption 3. The United States will encounter stiff resistence from Opposition parties, the media, and opponents of Prime Minister Nakasone in the LDP to proposals for greater military cooperation requiring large defense expenditures. The intensity of opposition will depend on the nature of the U.S. request.

Assumption 4. Such U.S. requests will provoke intense debate within the government and the Diet as Japan seeks to achieve a consensus on the extent of cooperation with the United States.

By listening more attentively to Japanese opinions, the United States will be better able to develop security proposals that will be acceptable to Japan. In developing and presenting these proposals, style is often as important as substance.

Public badgering of Japan creates deep resentment and solidifies opposition to the United States. A professional, business- like approach with proposals that are realistic and specific holds the most promise of a favorable reception. Emphasis on certain levels of spending in GNP terms will not be productive and will create confusion in the Japanese government.

By mutually examining how to share responsibilities more effectively in specific areas and by strengthening the forums for joint consultation, U.S.-Japan military cooperation will be enhanced. Already, significant progress has been made through joint military exercises, exchanges of information, by initiating a policy of technology transfer, and through joint development of strategy and tactics for air and sea surveillance. These efforts should be expanded. Japan's participation in the U.S. Strategic Defense Initiative (SDI) program, as I will note later, could provide further opportunities for defense collaboration.

Japanese accommodation to U.S. security requests and the process of incremental defense expansion in Japan should be studied carefully to determine in what ways the United States could assist the Japanese government in broadening its defense activities and how the Japanese could help in alleviating some of the security burdens carried by the United States in the Western Pacific.

The Japanese, in the past, have successfully managed the visits of U.S. nuclear-powered submarines and Japan's participation in RIMPAC exercises without significant political repercussions. Close U.S. cooperation with the Japanese government in these activities was important in denying the Opposition opportunities for mischief-making. Identifying the common features in these actions that allowed the Japanese government to carry-out policies without incurring serious political risks could provide important clues on how to bring Japan's defense effort more into line with the common objectives of both countries.

We should develop greater opportunities for joint consultation and involve Japan more, than in the past, in a wide range of bi-lateral, regional and global issues that concern the security of both countries. For example, we should broaden the Security Consultative Committee (SCC) concept, which has served as the focal point for U.S.-Japan defense discussions for several decades, to include not only Foreign Ministry and JDA officials who have traditionally been participants in SCC discussions, but officers from the Finance Ministry and the Ministry of International Trade and Industry as well.

A forum should also be created for media representatives from both countries to discuss security issues. The Japanese media exerts a powerful influence on public opinion and is an important force in shaping a consensus on the defense buildup.

A joint meeting of members of the secretariats of the Japan National Security Council and the U.S. National Security Council co-chaired by the heads of both organizations on a regular basis would expose the Japanese side to a review of American global commitments at a high policy level.

Liberal Democratic Party (LDP) leaders and key U.S. congressmen and Senators, especially those from the Armed Forces and Foreign Affairs Committees, should meet on an ad hoc basis to gain new perspectives on ways to strengthen defense cooperation.

The bureaucratic pitfalls in organizing such meetings should be faced squarely. Efforts should be made to accommodate to the particular bureaucratic traditions and styles of each country. Private funding should be sought for forums in which non-government individuals participate.

Ways must be found to create new Japanese perspectives on defense.

Defense spending is looked upon by the public as the price Japan must pay to maintain satisfactory relations with the United States. Until the Japanese see these defense outlays as being in Japan's national interest and not merely as a means to satisfy the United States, her defense program will continue to lag.

The United States must make a greater effort to understand the complexities of the Japanese security system and to improve the quality of U.S. representatives who negotiate with their Japanese counterparts. Learning more about the history and culture of Japan and gaining some proficiency in the Japanese language are essential.

Finally, we must define precisely what we mean by equity in burden sharing. For example, Japan could make a substantial contribution by making available to NATO countries her technology in missile tracking systems and heat resistent materials and could increase her aid to countries where the United States and Japan have strategic interests.

We have invited Japan to participate, along with our Western Allies, in the Strategic Defense Initiative Program. Japan could contribute to SDI through her advanced technology. In doing so, she could gain a deeper sense of sharing of the defense burden with the United States. While prospects of Japan joining SDI appear better than 50/50, there are problems. The public is concerned over a too close identification with the United States in any future U.S.-Soviet confrontation. There is an awareness of Japan's vulnerability to Soviet intimidation over a positive response to the United States. There is also the risk of alienating the United States over refusal to join SDI.

On the other hand, Japan realizes the technological advantages of cooperating in SDI research and the need to compete in the increasingly heated technological race. If Japan accepts the U.S. invitation to join SDI, her acceptance could be a vehicle for promoting closer and more effective U.S.-Japan defense cooperation and it would help in defining for Japan how greater parity in defense burden sharing could be achieved.

If we and the Japanese are able to move more confidently down the path of cooperation and understanding, tolerant of our differences and sympathetic to the constraints that influence our defense efforts, we can forge an alliance that will have a significant bearing on the maintenance of peace in Northeast Asia.

Research for this manuscript took place in Japan from February 2, 1985 to March 6, 1985 and from July 22, 1985 to August 25, 1985. The book is not an archival presentation, but rather an effort to give a contemporary perception of Japanese defense management through interviews with Japanese government officials and politicians having responsibility for defense policy, with academic and professional individuals who are influential in defense matters together with my interpretation and assessment of their views.

Those interviewed asked for anonymity and their wishes were honored. A list of those interviewed is in Appendix A. Statistics, tables, figures, and maps were largely drawn from official Japan Defense Agency publications.

Work in Japan culminated in a seminar held at International House, Tokyo on December 4, 1985, at which sixteen Japanese experts on defense discussed and debated in Japanese the security issue in Japanese politics, constraints on government efforts to improve the capability of the Self Defense Forces, and the role of the bureaucrat and politician in formulating the defense budget, the NDPO, and the MTPE. Special attention was given to what steps the United States should take to gain greater Japanese cooperation in defense burden sharing.

Most participants were critical of Japan's defense effort, of the role played by politicians and bureaucrats in shaping defense policy, of the effectiveness of the NDPO and the MTPE in creating an effective military force, of the media for distorting the true picture of Japan's security problems, and of the government for not providing the necessary leadership in defense policy. (Appendix F contains a complete text of the conference proceedings).

It is a pleasure to acknowledge the financial support given the research for this book by the Japan-United States Friendship Commission. I am especially indebted to friends in the ministries of Foreign Affairs and International Trade and Industry, in the Defense Agency and in the U.S. Embassy. To those in Japanese academia, the media and professional organizations who gave willingly of their time to patiently answer my questions, I am most grateful. To Dr. Howard Levy who spent long hours editing the original draft, to Mr. Raymond Aka of the American Embassy, Tokyo who gave invaluable help in arranging interviews, to Miss Kumie Kushizaki whose translations of important Japanese documents added a notable dimension to the research, and to my colleague at the Hoover Institution, Claude Buss, who offered thoughtful suggestions to strengthen the manuscript, I owe all a deep debt of gratitude.

The excellent East Asian Collection at the Hoover Institution and the rich library facilities at Stanford University were also a great help in preparing this book.

I wish to say something special about the contribution of Professor Kamata Shin'ichi of Japan's National Defense Academy to this manuscript. Professor Kamata was an indispensable source of information on the Japanese defense establishment. He spent many hours explaining the intricacies of decision-making within the Japan Defense Agency. It was especially important to have his explanation of how the budget was prepared and how the mid-term planning estimate was formulated. It would be hard to imagine how this book could have been completed without his help and support. While I am responsible for any errors that remain, the errors are undoubtedly less because of his assistance.

Introduction

Managing Japan's defense is a complicated and subtle business, made more so by the internal and external pressures on policymakers. Internally, the Japanese government must respond to a public which is satisfied with the slow, measured growth in the defense buildup program and desires military spending kept below 1% of the Gross National Product (GNP). Externally, Japan is receiving clear signals that the United States is impatient with the pace of Japan's defense program and urges a greater defense effort.

The dilemma implicit in these circumstances has compelled the Japanese government to design a defense budget and establish a National Defense Program Outline, NDPO, and a new (1985) Mid-Term Planning Estimate, MTPE, that seek a middle ground in the defense debate, a growth pattern that does not alarm the Japanese public while at the same time keeping the U.S.-Japan defense relationship in some equilibrium.

Bureaucrats and politicians involved in the management of Japan's defense must be continually aware of these pressures and counter-pressures, especially during the preparation of the defense budget, and as efforts go forward to comply with the guidelines of the NDPO and the MTPE.

Their responsibilities take on greater urgency as Soviet military power continues to grow in the Western Pacific. Yet, they are circumscribed by the realities of the defense issue in Japanese politics. Why Japan seems unable to assume more responsibility for her own defense, why the Japanese have mandated a slow, measured buildup of their military forces despite U.S. urgings for a greater defense effort, why the United States has been unable to substantially influence the scope and pace of the Japanese defense buildup, and how the Japanese are dealing with their defense dilemma are questions that will be addressed.

The main focus will be on the defense budget, NDPO, and MTPE, examining how the annual budget is prepared in the face of demanding pressures from inside and outside Japan, and how the NDPO and MTPE are interpreted by government officials and politicians as they attempt to placate the foes of a greater defense effort on the one hand and a frustrated United States on the other. It requires subtlety and finesse, and sofar the Japanese seem to have been able to steer a successful middle course. But the status quo so zealously advocated by most Japanese is beginning to show signs of wear.

Japan and the United States are entering the last half of the 1980s with the problem of burden-sharing largely unresolved. While there has been considerable progress in U.S.-Japan military cooperation, frustration, uncertainty, and complacency best describe the mood at policy levels.

Japan's defense policy is based on the premise that Japan is not threatened by anyone and therefore need not increase its military strength at a pace that would impinge on economic development or the "comfortable life" increasingly enjoyed by the Japanese people. A complicating factor is that Japan views its defense strategy in regional terms whereas the United States looks upon its security interest in global dimensions. Important political, economic, and social constraints that restrict the flexibility of Japanese leaders further compounds the problem.

Prime Minister Nakasone Yasuhiro and the leaders of the ruling Liberal Democratic Party (LDP) are inhibited in their efforts to improve Japanese defense capabilities by a Constitution whose Article 9 stipulates that war can no longer be an instrument of national policy; by an austere national budget that has seriously cut back on government spending; by a National Defense Program Outline that fails to address some of the important strategic and tactical policy questions, merely setting broad guidelines for force levels, maintenance, and improvement of defense facilities, weapons procurement, and research and development; by a calculated concern over the reaction of Japan's neighbors to an ambitious defense program; by the relative weakness of the Japan Defense Agency in its contest with more powerful bureaucracies; and by a public that fears resurgent militarism, is deeply pacifist, and opposes excessive spending for defense. These are formidable obstaclesa and should be understood for what they are - the principal reasons for the slow growth of Japanese military strength.

Although both countries disagree on the pace of the Japanese defense buildup, they do agree that Japan should not become a regional or major military power but only reach a level in her rearmament effort to allow for more equitable burden-sharing with the United States. Successive American administrations have supported such a policy.

The U.S.-Japan alliance has important strengths. The two countries form the principal cornerstone of economic development in the region and with American military power and Japan's strategic location, the principal safeguard for political stability and peace in the Western Pacific. Their security relationship is anchored in the U.S.-Japan Security Treaty, an arrangement that has served the common interests of both countries for the past three decades. It has given the Japanese a chance to rebuild their war-shattered economy into the second most powerful one in the Free World and has provided the United States with key military bases that have helped stabilize security conditions in the Western Pacific.

Yet the United States remains dissatisfied with several aspects\ of Japanese defense policy. Since gaining independence from Allied Occupation in 1952, Japan has taken pains to emphasize the defense nature of her security policy. The three non-nuclear principles, laws prohibiting arms sales and the development of offensive weapons, limiting defense spending to no more than 1% of the Gross National Product, establishing the National Defense Program Outline in 1976 which stressed the peaceful nature of Japanese foreign policy and placed limits on Japan's defense buildup - all form an integral part of Japan's security doctrine. Efforts by the United States to persuade Japan to expand her defense program; to share the defense burden more equitably; to participate with the United States in a broader collective security role in East Asia - all have been met with polite rejection. Japanese leaders explain that their Constitution makes explicit the requirement to avoid a strategic role for Japan in the Western Pacific. They also point to the U.S.-Japan Mutual Security Treaty as further evidence of U.S. acceptence of Japanese security policy.

Despite these assertions, there are stirrings on both sides of the Pacific that the Treaty should be more balanced; that Japan should take on more responsibilities for her own defense, befitting a nation with a powerful economy.

Some Japanese leaders and high defense officials, retired and on active duty, are talking privately about the need to revise Article 5 of the Mutual Security Treaty, which calls for the United States to come to the defense of

Japan in case of attack but places no similar obligation on Japan if the United States were attacked in places other than territories under Japanese administration, to allow Japan to cooperate more closely with the United States when Japan or the United States are threatened. These officials also believe a more liberal interpretation of Article 6 of the Treaty which allows U.S. military forces to use bases in Japan would help to forestall aggression against either party. These private airings are not necessarily in accord with current public opinion but are being voiced with increasing frequency. Security officials contend that the public can be better educated to recognize that close U.S.-Japan military cooperation is in Japan's vital security interests.

While U.S. officials have long wanted Japan to strengthen its defense forces and provide a more liberal policy on U.S. use of Japanese bases, the use of these facilities must be managed within the context of political realities in Japan. There are also those who worry about the resurgence of Japanese militarism and contend that close cooperation between the two countries on security policy will tend to prevent such an occurance.

As time passes and security conditions in East Asia change, both sides will likely increase their interest in how the Mutual Security Treaty can be modified to better safeguard the security interests of Japan and the United States.

The task remains to work for the alleviation of misunderstandings and to deepen cooperation. An important first step is to study the influence and responsibilities of the bureaucrat and politician in defense policy decision-making and how these policymakers make the necessary adjustments in the budget and in interpretations of the NDPO and the MTPE to deal with the dilemma facing Japan in her defense policy. Understanding how these officials operate will provide important clues to U.S. policymakers on ways to gain greater Japanese support in burden sharing. Considerable attention will therefore be given to the roles of bureaucrats and politicians in defining defense policies within the Japanese government and the Liberal Democratic Party and to a description of some of the key managers in the defense policy structure and their influence in allocating resources for the defense buildup.

Current Japanese defense policies can be traced back to the early 1950s when the Japan Defense Agency (JDA) was established and the political framework for the defense debate set. This study will therefore begin with an examination of defense organization, the institutional framework within which the bureaucrat and politician must work in managing defense, highlighting the Prime Minister's Office and the National Defense Council and JDA which are a part of that office.

The origin and evolution of the JDA, its powerful internal bureaus, (naikyoku), the military components, the influence of the Constitution, and pertinent laws and regulations on the organization and policies of the agency will be examined.

The Diet, particularly Liberal Democratic Party Committees that are involved in defense matters will be reviewed.

With this institutional framework as background, the study will move to defense operations, the constraints on defense policy, the relations between civilians and military personnel in the formulation and execution of defense programs, the need to build a career civilian cadre in the JDA, and the agency's relations with other government departments such as the ministries of Finance, Foreign Affairs, and International Trade and Industry.

The study will next turn to the NDPO, regarded as the blueprint for Japan's defense buildup yet considered by most experts as merely the charter for the acquisition of weapon systems. Weapons purchases under the NDPO are generally unrelated to specific military missions.

The NDPO establishes the objectives for Japan's defense program, examines the international situation in 1976 but with no provision for an analysis of the present state of international affairs, establishes the basic concept and posture of national defense, the role of the Ground, Maritime, and Air Self Defense Forces, and outlines basic policy for the defense buildup. (See Apopendix E for the text of the National Defense Program Outline.)

The NDPO was established in 1976 at a time when detente was a fashionable word and Japan could devise a defense program based upon the presumed lessening of tensions between the Soviet Union and the United States. The doctrine is out of date, appears immune, at least for the present, to change or modification, yet it continues to form the guidelines for todays's defense buildup. The study will discuss the origins of the NDPO, principal features and accomplishments and prospects for change, and its impact on the defense budget and defense planning.

Another major element in the study of Japanese security management is the Mid-Term Planning Estimate. The history of the MTPE, its influence on the defense budget, and its effectiveness in meeting Japan's security needs are important factors for evaluating the Japanese defense effort.

In September 1985, the MTPE took on added significance in the form of a new 5-year Plan and became official government policy. Before, the MTPE was only an internal planning instrument of the JDA. The implications of the new MTPE for Japanese defense policy will be carefully appraised.

With the fundamental policies of the NDPO and the MTPE in mind, the study will next center on what many experts consider the key to understanding Japanese defense policy, the defense budget process. This process is an enigma cloaked in vagueness and ambiguity where logic seems to have little relevance. Yet it is critically important to penetrate this labyrinth in order to understand how spending limits are set and resources allocated to meet the conflicting pressures faced by policymakers.

The commitment given the United States by Japan that it will assume air and sea surveillance responsibility for an area 1000 miles from Japan is an example of such conflicting considerations. For example, when Prime Minister Suzuki Zenko visited President Reagan in Washington in May 1981, he assured Mr. Reagan, among other things, that the Japanese would undertake the defense of Japan to 1000 miles from the home islands. The President was delighted and he and Defense Department officials had high expectations for an early realization of Mr. Suzuki's promise. The reality was quite different. The Japanese Defense Agency studied the Prime Minister's statement to Mr. Reagan and is still mulling it over, still uncertain how to develop and implement a policy that has an unknown price tag and important legal ramifications. Meanwhile the Pentagon fumes.

The defense budget, which is our main concern here, will be viewed from several perspectives. First, the major components of the budget will be studied and the budget as a reflection of national priorities and problems in budget management will be examined. The study will take a close look at the participants in the budget process, discussing the human factor in budget decision-making and identifying the key managers.

Another perspective in which to view the budget process is to examine the policy of capping defense spending at 1% of the Gross National Product and study the consequences of this action. The policy has been in effect for nearly a decade and in the opinion of many experts has seriously eroded the defense buildup. The 1% policy will be discussed in terms of its origin, its impact on the defense budget and Japan's military capabilities, its utilization by the media and others opposed to a stepped-up defense effort, and the prospects for change.

In order to examine the interaction of bureaucrat and politician in the budget process and how conflicting pressures are handled, I present a case study of the 1985 defense budget, showing the schedule for budget preparation and providing some observations on the mechanics of budget formulation.

Finally, the dilemma in Japanese security management must be viewed in the context of bureaucratic and political action. The military services, JDA and the ministries of Finance, Foreign Affairs, and International Trade and industry consider the practical issues of the defense budget, operational plans, force objectives, establishment of resource priorities and personnel and equipment requirements. Politically, LDP members, especially major faction leaders, the Secretary General of the LDP, the chairmen of the Executive Council and the Policy Affairs Research Council of the party, the Chief Cabinet Secretary and the Prime Minister are all involved in making a final determination on the ultimate spending level for the defense budget. In doing so, they are sensitive not only to domestic considerations but to pressures from the United States.

The defense budget, the NDPO, and the MTPE form the tripod that supports Japanese defense policy. Understanding the interaction of these three elements, the role of the politician and bureaucrat in the process, and how policy adjustments are made to satisfy the main constituents of that policy, the Japanese public and the United States, and the many constraints on Japan's leaders which make it difficult for them to respond more postively to American urgings for a greater defense effort, are vital if American policymakers are to be more successful in gaining Japanese support for a more equitable sharing of the defense burden.

Chapter 1

Defense Organization

The Prime Minister's Office; National Defense Council; Defense Agency

The Prime Minister is the pivotal official in all matters of defense, the commander-in-chief of the SDF yet one whose influence is sometimes marginal on critical defense issues because of the diffusion of responsibility in the government leadership. In most cases, he is more a chairman of the board than a leader whose decision is final and authority unquestioned.

The Chief Cabinet Secretary in the Prime Minister's Office coordinates defense policy. He is considered the righthand of the Prime Minister and is in constant touch with senior party leaders, the Secretary General of the LDP, the chiefs of the Executive Council and the Policy Affairs Research Council and key government officials and Dietmen who are involved in defense policy. Former Chief Cabinet Secretary, Fujinami Takao of the Nakasone faction, played an important part in trying to convince senior faction leaders (without success) to agree to remove the 1% cap on defense spending. His task and those of other high government officials and leading LDP politicians become exceedingly important during annual summer/fall negotiations over the defense budget, consideration of the 1% ceiling issue and defense problems associated with the NDPO and the MTPE.

The National Defense Council, authorized by Article 62 of the Defense Agency Establishment Law of 1954 and established in 1956, includes the Prime Minister, Foreign Minister, Finance Minister, Director General of the Defense Agency, and Director General of the Economic Planning Agency. (See Appendix C).

Other regular attendees are the Minister of International Trade and Industry, the Director General of the Science and Technology Agency, the Chief Cabinet Secretary, and the Secretary General of the NDC Secretariat. The latter is assisted by a staff of up to nine counsellors and other staff members totalling 27 personnel. All are civilians. The Prime Minister also invites other parties to attend NDC sessions as the situation requires.

The Chairman of the military Joint Staff Council is asked to speak only when there is a need and only at the discretion of the Prime Minister.

There are presently (April 1985) eight counsellors of whom five represent the five permanent agencies on the NDC. They meet infrequently and while technically part of the Secretariat, the five have their own offices and responsibilities in their parent agencies. The MITI representative, for example, is Chief of the Defense Industries and Aircraft Division of MITI and devotes practically all of his time to his division duties.

The NDC is scheduled to meet twice a year but in some years it has not met at all. The infrequency of meetings is testimony to its questionable influence in the defense decision-making process.

On July 22,1985, the Special Advisory Committee on Administrative

1

Reform headed by the distinguished business patriarch, Doko Toshiwo, recommended to the government that the National Defense Council be reorganized into the National Security Council with "teeth" to promote better defense management and assure continued civilian control.

According to *Nihon Keizai* of October 30,1985, Prime Minister Nakasone, at a meeting of the Lower House Budget Committee on October 29, said that the government and the LDP were working on legislative proposals to reorganize the NDC into a National Security Council. He also voiced support for upgrading the Lower House Special Security Committee to a standing committee of the Diet.

During the same Diet session, General Affairs Agency Director General Gotoda Masaharu noted that reorganization of the NDC was premised on the need to strengthen civilian control of military affairs. Under the reorganization plan, Gotoda said that the National Security Council would be composed of the Prime Minister as Chairman, the Foreign Minister, Finance Minister, Chief Cabinet Secretary, Director General of the Defense Agency, and the Chairman of the National Public Safety Commission. The latter would be a new addition to the NSC while the Director General of the Economic Planning Agency would be dropped from membership.

At the same time, the NDC Secretariat would be abolished and a "Security Room" established in the Cabinet Secretariat to be headed by an official of Vice Ministerial rank. The new NSC would thus become an organ directly subordinated to the Cabinet, which was not the case with the NDC, with greatly enhanced authority.

In the past, other attempts have been made to restructure the NDC but support from key politicians in the LDP and from the ministries of Finance and International Trade and Industry has not been forthcoming. However, with strong support from the Doko Commission and Prime Minister Nakasone, the government introduced legislation in the April 1986 Diet session to reorganize the NDC. The legislative proposal, known as the Security Council Establishment Bill, was approved by the Diet in May 1986. The National Defense Council Establishment Law must now be amended to implement the new NSC law.

Under Japan's parliamentary system, the present NDC has been a special clearing house for defense matters. The law stipulates that the NDC must approve long-range planning, the budget, and major equipment purchases. For example, the JDA must formally present its budget, procurement plans, and long and medium range defense needs to the NDC. Yet, in the opinion of most Japanese defense experts, the NDC is more a facilitator than a primary actor in defense policy. The sum of its parts carries less weight and influence in the defense policy process than its individual members. Many of the issues that the NDC is asked to formally decide upon have already been settled through coordination among concerned bureaucrats and politicians. The head of the new NSC, Sassa Atsuyuki, a former high official of the JDA, has emphasized to the *Japan Times* that the NSC would not have any decision-making powers but would coordinate different points of view on defense policy. It is therefore probable that the new NSC, while stronger than its predecessor, will still have to submit to the traditional ways of doing business in the Japanese bureaucracy.

Japan Defense Agency - Origin and Evolution

Historical Background

The JDA's origin was intimately linked to the creation of the Self Defense Forces and to American occupation policy. The primary objective of that policy was demilitarization and democratization. Article 9 of the Japanese Constitution gave further support to these American policy objectives by declaring that "... aspiring sincerely to an international peace based on justice and order, the Japanese people forever renounce war as a sovereign right of the nation and the threat of force as a means of settling disputes. In order to accomplish the aim...,land, sea and air forces, as well as other war potential, will never be maintained. The right of belligerency of the State will not be recognized."

Early American policy was also based upon the prospect of Sino-Soviet-American cooperation in post-war Asia. As the Cold War approached and East-West relations worsened, Occupation goals shifted and began to emphasize rapid economic growth and early Japanese independence. At the outbreak of the Korean War in June 1950, the United States sent four American divisions stationed in Japan to Korea. To replace them, General Douglas MacArthur ordered the Japanese Goverenment to establish a National Police Reserve Force of 75,000 men.

In his letter to Prime Minister Yoshida Shigeru dated July 8, 1950, General MacArthur said, "In keeping with my established policy to re-invest autonomous authority in the Japanese Government as rapidly as the situation permits, I have visualized the progressive development of law enforcing agencies adequate to the maintenance of internal security and order and the safeguard of Japan's coastline against unlawful immigration and smuggling.

"By letter of September 16,1947, I approved the recommendation of the Japanese Goverenment for an increase in the overall strength of Japan's police force to 125,000 men, making provision for a new national rural police force of 30,000 men. It was then the view of the government, in which I fully concurred, that the strength recommended and authorized was not an arbitrary determination of future police requirements but designed to provide an adequate force around which might be built a modern and democratic police system oriented to an effective decentralization of the policy responsibility in harmony with the constitutional principle of local autonomy.

"Subsequent action in the recruitment, equipping and training of the police force then authorized has proceeded with commendable efficiency. The concept of autonomous responsibility has been faithfully observed, essential coordination has been carefully developed and the proper relationship between the police and private citizenry has been progressively forged. As a consequence, the Japanese people today may take justifiable pride in this agency for the enforcement of law at all levels of government. Indeed, it may be credited to both organizational police efficiency and the law-abiding character of the Japanese people that, despite a much lower police strength in relation to population here than is to be found in most of the other democratic states and the general post-war impoverishment and other adverse conditions usually conducive to lawlessness, Japan stands out with a calmness and serenity which lends emphasis to the violence, confusion and disorder which exists in other nearby lands. "To ensure that this favorable condition will continue unchallenged by lawless minorities, here as elsewhere committed to the subversion of the due processes of law and assaults of opportunity against the peace and public welfare, I believe that the police system has reached that degree of efficiency in organization and training which will permit its augmentation to a strength which will bring it within the limits experience has shown to be essential to the safeguard of the public welfare in a democratic society.

"Insofar as maritime safety in the harbors and coastal waters of Japan is concerned the Maritime Safety Board has achieved highly satisfactory results but events disclose that safeguard of the long Japanese coastal line against unlawful

3

immigration and smuggling activity requires employment of a larger force under this agency than is presently provided for by law.

"Accordingly, I authorize your government to take the necessary measures to establish a national police reserve of 75,000 men and expand the existing authorized strength of the personnel serving under the Maritime Safety Board by an additional 8,000. the current year's operating cost of these increments to existing agencies may be made available from funds previously allocated in the General Account of the National Budget toward retirement of the public debt. The appropriate sections of this Headquarters will be available, as heretofore, to advise and assist in the technical aspects of these measures."

"Very Sincerely,

(sgd)

"Douglas MacArthur" 1.

This was the nucleus of what later became the SDF. It also ushered in the era of the defense debate. For the next few years the defense issue was hotly argued in Japan. Gradually the Japanese moved toward establishing a legal framework for the defense establishment and in 1954 after lengthy negotiations among political parties the government submitted two defense laws to the Diet, the Defense Agency Establishment Law and the Self Defense Force Law. Both were passed on June 2,1954 and the JDA and the SDF were formally established. (See Appendix B.)

The enactment of these two laws began a prolonged period of fierce political and academic contention over the legality of the SDF. The Defense Agency became the unwilling target of much of the skirmishing. For members of the SDF, it was an especially troublesome time. Much of the public was hostile to the men in uniform, often accusing them of being "tax robbers." The situation reached a point where military personnel would change into civilian clothes before leaving the base. Civilian recruitment for the JDA also suffered because of public suspicions of the military.

Since then, the Self Defense Forces and the Defense Agency have worked quietly to improve their image. They have reached a level of public acceptance that could not have been forecast a decade or two ago. The Agency, however, continues to worry over budget problems and the SDF to fret about a dominant civilian bureaucracy, an absence of laws and regulations to cover emergency military situations and obscure and ambivalent military doctrine.

Present Organization

The JDA is comprised of the Internal Bureaus (*naikyoku*), Ground, Maritime and Air Staff Offices, the Joint Staff Council, the Defense Facilities Administrative Agency and various other units and organizations. Figure 1 is a diagram of the Defense Agency.

Figure 1. Outline of Organization of Defense Agency and SDF

(As of July 1, 1986)

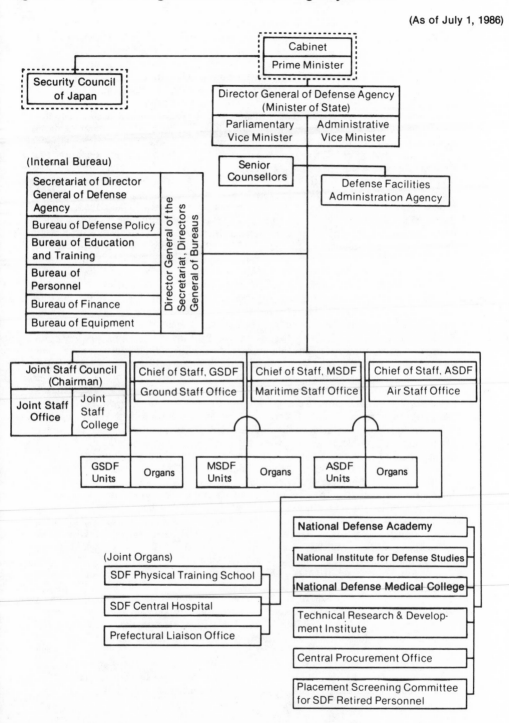

Source: Defense of Japan, 1986. Japan Defense Agency

The Internal Bureaus constitute the center of power within the JDA and are the main instrument by which civilian control of the military establishment is realized. The Bureau directors meet once or twice a week with four senior counsellors, the Administrative Vice Minister and the Director General of the JDA at what is called the Counsellor's Council. Uniformed officers from the Joint Staff Council (equivalent to the U.S. Joint Chiefs of Staff) attend some of the Council meetings but only in the role of technical experts to be called upon to answer specific questions. The bureaus are staffed by civilian professionals who make all the important decisions subject to approval of the Director General or his principal deputy. Chiefs of the most important bureaus are officials drawn from other ministries. There are only about 500 authorized positions in the Internal Bureaus, 150 of which are slated for civilian defense planners, the key officials who must deal with the three military services, other ministries and the Diet. Equally disturbing to careerists is the lack of a clear policy in the JDA to promote a career official to the top position in the Agency. The JDA has some distance to travel before its career officers can seriously challenge seconded officials for the top posts in the Internal Bureaus. Figure 2 is a diagram of classification and numbers of personnel of the JDA. Figure 3 is a diagram of the Internal Bureaus.

The Defense Policy, Finance, and Equipment bureaus are three powerful units within the Internal Bureaus. The Defense Policy Bureau is first among equals and has the responsibility for drafting defense policy, defense buildup programs, operational activities of the SDF and information gathering and analysis. The Bureau is presently (April 1985) headed by an official of the Finance Ministry. The Defense Section of the Bureau, the principal liaison point with the three military services, has units staffed with civilians to deal with their counterparts in the Ground, Maritime and Air Self Defense Forces.

The Finance Bureau, headed by a Finance Ministry official, plays a crucial role in the development of the JDA budget and establishes spending priorities for the JDA and the SDF. Like the Defense Policy Bureau, it has sub-units whose personnel deal directly in budget preparation with their military opposites in the Ground, Maritime and Air Self Defense Forces. Finance Bureau officials maintain close contact with their colleagues in the Finance Ministry exchanging opinions and information as budget negotiations proceed.

The Equipment Bureau has an important role in equipment procurement for the three military services. Headed by a senior official of the Ministry of International Trade and Industry, (MITI), it is also organized in sub-units to deal directly with the three military services. MITI officials keep in close touch with the Director General of the Equipment Bureau on all issues involving planning and purchase of military hardware. The sub-units are in contact with their counterparts in the military services in order to work out a consensus on procurement policy and specific procurement items.

For example, if the ASDF wishes to introduce a sophisticated communication system in their aircraft, the recommendation first goes to the Defense Policy Bureau where a determination is made from a policy point of view whether to adopt such a system. If the bureau agrees that the system should be incorporated into ASDF aircraft, the issue then goes to the Equipment and Finance bureaus to decide what kind of system should be purchased (Equipment) and how it should be funded (Finance).

The Internal Bureaus are the axis of the JDA; they constitute the stronghold of the civilian bureaucrats who develop defense policy, manage the defense budget and establish priorities for the procurement of military

Figure 2.
Classification and Numbers of Personnel of the JDA

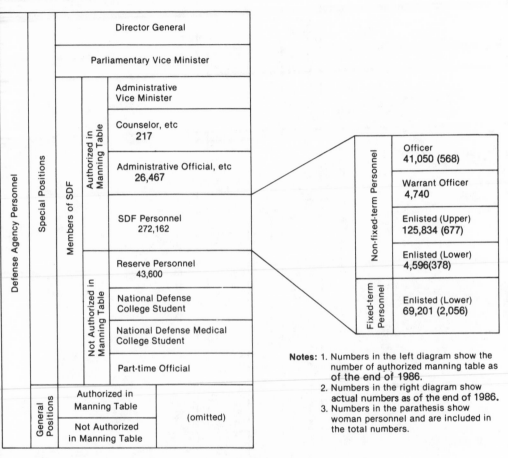

Notes:
1. Numbers in the left diagram show the number of authorized manning table as of the end of 1986.
2. Numbers in the right diagram show actual numbers as of the end of 1986.
3. Numbers in the parathesis show woman personnel and are included in the total numbers.

Source: Defense of Japan, 1986. Japan Defense Agency

Figure 3
Internal Bureaus (NAIKYOKU)

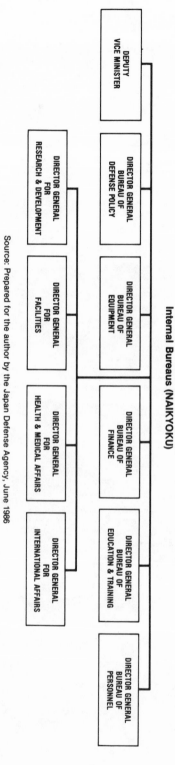

Source: Prepared for the author by the Japan Defense Agency, June 1986

equipment. Through their links with the Finance Ministry, MITI, the Prime Ministers's Office, the Foreign Ministry and key LDP Diet members, these civilian professionals produce a budget that provides for the essential needs of the SDF yet allows for political decisions that meet the broader requirements of the Japanese Government, especially those having an impact on defense relations with the United States.

The Diet - Liberal Democratic Party Committees

The main factions in the LDP (Abe, Tanaka, Miyazawa, and Nakasone) tend to mirror divergent views present in Japanese society on defense policy. These opinions range from advocacy of the status quo by the mainline factions of the Party to the more hawkish views of Mr. Nakasone and such senior LDP politicians as Fujinami, former Education Minister Fujii, and past Directors General of the JDA, Kanemaru, Mihara, Yamashita, Omura, and Ito. It is generally conceded that over 50% of the public is in the "status quo" category and most of the LDP faction members reflect this position. The Socialists, Komeito, the Communists and to a lesser degree the Democratic Socialists are usually opposed to any efforts to accelerate the defense buildup.

To handle defense problems more effectively, especially issues generated by U.S. demands for a greater Japanese defense effort, the LDP agreed in 1980 to organize special committees on defense to provide a broader forum for party discussion. It was hoped that debate within these committees would eventually lead to a consensus on security problems. Decisions could then flow upward in the LDP structure where they would eventually reach the Policy Affairs Research Council (PARC) and the Executive Council.

Within the PARC, various interest groups, civil servants, and elected officials converge to discuss and negotiate policy concerns. According to LDP by-laws, all matters relevant to policy affairs must first be examined by the PARC. The policies approved by the PARC are then sent to the Executive Council for final approval prior to being brought to the Diet for legislative deliberation.

In normal situations, policy matters initiated by the bureaucrats are referred to one of the seventeen divisions - *bukai*- of the PARC that are organized to parallel the standing committees of the Diet. Management of these seventeen divisions is under the direct influence of the concerned LDP-controlled ministries and agencies, just as the individual standing committees of both houses of the Diet are influenced by individual ministries and agencies. For example, a special relationship exists between the national defense division of the PARC and the Defense Agency.

Other sub committee groups within the PARC (i.e. Security Affairs Research Council, Base Measures Special Committee, the Foreign Affairs Research Council, and the Defense Power Consolidation Sub Committee) also influence defense policy. 2.

By virtue of their long tenure, some LDP members are able to accumulate impressive knowledge on specific policy topics through membership on the PARC committees. In this way a close relationship is built by a conservative politician with both bureaucrats and special interest groups. The pattern has been labeled by the Japanese media as *zoku* politics. Influential members of the *zoku* group, in addition to those already mentioned, are Shiina Motoo, Kato Koichi, Tsukihara Higehiro, Arima Motoji, and Miyashita, Suihei. See figure 4 for the organizational structure of the PARC.

These sub forums exist within the Policy Affairs Research Council and include the National Defense Division, the Security Affairs Research Council, the

Base Measures Special Committee and the Foreign Affairs Research Council. Satellite committees also exist such as the Defense Power Consolidation Sub Committee.

The relatively new Diet Comprehensive Security Parliamentarians Consultative Council, has representatives from Komeito, the Democratic Socialist Party, the New Liberal Club as well as the sponsoring LDP, provides a structure for discussion of Japanese security issues by diverse groups. This broad multi-party representation in a Diet committee reflects the gradual change that is taking place in the defense environment toward greater acceptance of the importance of defense in government policy.

The often doctrinaire Socialist Party that earlier advocated the abolishment of the SDF and a policy of "positive neutrality" has moved to a more pragmatic position despite the efforts of its left-wing faction to contest the trend. Party members with a special interest in defense matters are Ueda Tetsu, Kawakami Tamio, Uehara Yasusuke, and Inaba Seiichi. Many defense analysts believe that the Socialist Party's overall influence in defense policy is weakening.

LDP Diet members who tend to gravitate toward membership in defense-related committees have relatively little influence in policy councils. None is especially influential in the Party, none has supporting organizations nor the backing of leaders of major factions. As these pro-defense party members seek to gain further support for a more active defense buildup by joining these defense committees, their "hawkish" stance tends to diminish the effectiveness of their efforts.

Figure 4. Policy Affairs Research Council of the Liberal Democratic Party

Source: Japan Economic Survey, December 1986.

The interaction of defense committee members, concerned bureaucrats, and local officials who deal with issues, especially those affecting the operation of U.S. forces in Japan, is especially instructive. In these meetings, efforts are made to cope with the dilemma facing defense policymakers - a skeptical Japanese public and a demanding U.S. government. I will cite examples of such interaction and the pressures on participants in Chapter 5, The Defense Budget Process. Meanwhile the forums for discussing U.S.-Japan security problems are diagrammed in Figure 5.

Figure 5. Major Forums for Japan-U.S. Consultations on Security

(As of March 31, 1985)

Japanese side	Legal basis	Consultative forum	Purpose	U.S. side
Minister of Foreign Affairs, Director General of the Defense Agency, and others	Established on the basis of letters exchanged between the Prime Minister of Japan and the U.S. Secretary of State Jan. 19, 1950 in accordance with Article IV of Secretary Treaty	Security Consultative Committee	Study of matters which would promote understanding between the Japanese and U.S. governments and contribute to the strengthening of cooperative relations in the area of security and which forms the basis of security and are related to security	U.S. Ambassador to Japan, Commander of the U.S. Pacific Command (Proxy: commander of U.S. Forces in Japan, and others)
Participants not specified meetings held from time to time between working-level officials of the two governments such as officials corresponding in rank to vice minister or undersecretary	Article IV of Security Treaty	Security Subcommittee	Exchange of view on security issues of common concern to Japan and the U.S.	Participants not specified meetings held from time to time between working-level officials of the two governments such as officials corresponding in rank to vice minister or undersecretary
Deputy Vice Minister for Foreign Affairs, Director General of North American Affairs Bureau, Ministry of Foreign Affairs, Director General of Defense Facilities Administration Agency, Director General, Bureau of Defense Policy, Defense Agency Chairman of Joint Staff Council and others	Established on the basis of the agreement reached between the Minister of Foreign Affairs and the U.S. Ambassador to Japan Jan. 19, 1973 in accordance with Article IV Security Treaty	Security Consultative Group	Consultation and coordination concerning operation of Security Treaty and related arrangements	Minister and Counsellor at the U.S. Embassy Commander and Chief of Staff of U.S. Forces, Japan, and others
Director General of North American Affairs Bureau, Ministry of Foreign Affairs, Director General of Defense Facilities Administration Agency, and others.	Article XXV of Status of Forces Agreement	Japan-U.S. Joint Committee (Once every two weeks in principle)	Consultation concerning implementations of Status of Forces Agreement	Chief of Staff of U.S. Forces, Japan, Counsellor at the U.S. Embassy, and others

Source: Defense of Japan, 1985. Defense Agency

Source: Defense of Japan, 1985. Japan Defense Agency

12

Chapter 2

Defense Operations

Constitution and Pertinent laws

The Constitution, and to a lesser degree the U.S.-Japan Mutual Security Treaty, have set the tone and direction for Japanese security and have been important constraints in building the SDF. The Constitution's clear message is peace; a Japan without offensive military forces, Japan dedicated to the resolution of international disputes through peaceful means, wishing to live and let live in the international community, and seeking a better life for her people through economic progress not military aggrandizement. It is a national policy consistent in purpose and steadfastly pursued by all post-war Japanese governments.

The Mutual Security Treaty and Article 9 of the Constitution renouncing war as an instrument of national policy have discouraged Japanese leaders from thinking in terms of a strategic or collective security role for Japan. These two fundamental documents have played a critical part in Japanese defense policy and have helped to foster a climate of unreality and a stubborn reluctance to change with an ever changing international environment. Working in such an atmosphere has made it difficult for the SDF and the JDA to carry out the responsibilities stipulated in the Self Defense Forces Law and the Defense Agency Establishment Law.

The Constitution has spawned several other laws affecting Japanese security that have left their imprint on defense policy. First was the Basic Policies for National Defense enacted in 1975 which, among other things, directed that a minimum self-defense capability necessary to assure Japan's freedom and security should be achieved. Unfortunately, the Basic Policies Law did not define what would be a minimum self-defense capability or how it could be attained.

Second was the National Defense Program Outline, NDPO, promulgated in 1976 which will be discussed in Chapter 3.

The SDF and the JDA have been especially troubled by the absence of laws and regulations covering emergency military situations within Japan. To carry out their responsibilities, the SDF believe they need authority to allow for unrestricted movement of SDF units in areas where local and national laws and regulations now govern the activities of individuals and institutions (i.e. the Road Law, Coastal Law, Forests and Woods Law, Construction and Standards Law, the Medical Care Law and the Law Governing Graveyards).

Use of coastal areas, forests and national parks, and the construction and repair of buildings, bridges and roads are all subject to these laws, which apply to the SDF as well as to the general public.

These circumstances prompted the JDA to submit a report to the Diet Special Committee on Security on October 16, 1984 proposing that certain laws be enacted to ensure smooth operation and mobilization of the SDF in time of emergency. Because these proposals contained recommendations that would allow

13

for unrestricted movement of SDF units and involve expropriation of land, transportation of material and storage of ammunition, they were judged too politically controversial by the Special Committee on Security.

The Socialist Party was hostile and the media skeptical and this led the government and the LDP to move cautiously in considering the issue.

It has now been shelved, but most defense experts with whom I talked admitted that if the SDF had to obtain prior permission to make urgent repairs on damaged roads and bridges, build field hospitals, bury the dead or set up field command posts in potential battle zones, their ability to carry out their defense mission would be seriously affected.

It would take considerable effort by the national government, analysts believe, to obtain public acceptence of these emergency legislative proposals. Meanwhile the lack of such legislation constitutes another obstacle in the way of an effective defense buildup.

Policy Constraints Hindering Defense Operations

There are other constraints on Japan's defense buildup that portend even more serious problems for Japanese defense policy.

One is Japan's delicate financial situation. For several years the country has been living with an austere national budget and despite urgings from some members of the LDP, it is unlikely that financial restrictions imposed by an exacting fiscal policy will be eased appreciably. (Japan's cumulative budget deficit is now (August 1986) nearing $600 billion or about 40% of the GNP.)

There has not been enough money in the defense budget over the past several years to begin to remedy the shortage of ammunition, spare parts and petroleum capacity; or the weaknesses in logistics and communication that encumber the military; or the obsolescence of most artillery anti-tank weapons and tanks that reduce the capability of the armed forces. The allocation of funds for new equipment for the Maritime, Air and Ground Self Defense Forces has not been adequate to implement the NDPO.

In May, 1984, the Japanese Government conceded that it would be unable to meet the timetable for a defense buildup and had to approve a three-year delay in the rearmament program, pushing back completion until 1991 of a plan whereby weapons which were to be acquired and in operation by 1988 would merely be purchased.

Another limitation on the defense buildup is the absence of a realistic blueprint for defense policy. The NDPO was developed at a time of detente when there was much wishful thinking in Japan about an era of peace between the Soviet Union and the United States. Japanese leaders believed that they could devise a less ambitious defense program based upon a presumed lessening of world-wide tensions. The NDPO has proved, however, to be out of date yet it continues to form the strategic guidelines for today's (Sept. 1985) defense planning.

A third constraint on the defense buildup is the vulnerability of the Defense Agency itself. In the tough bureaucratic world of Japanese politics, the JDA cannot compete with the powerful Finance Ministry, the Ministry of International Trade and Industry and the Foreign Ministry for influence in defense policy.

Constitutional and legal restrictions, as we have noted, are also a handicap to those advocating a more forceful defense program. An effort to remove Article 9 of the Constitution or its reinterpretation would run the risk of losing what public consensus has been achieved within Japan for support of the SDF. Any efforts to reinterpret Article 9 to allow more flexibility in Japan's defense planning will take time to gain acceptence.

Another restraint on defense operations is the concern in Japan about the reaction of Japan's neighbors to an ambitious defense program. While opinions differ in ASEAN countries and in China and Korea about Japanese rearmament, a common concern in these countries is that Japan not become a regional military power. Paradoxically, Japan often plays on this sentiment to justify the modest nature of its own defense effort.

A further limiting factor on the defense buildup is the perception held by Japanese regarding the Soviet threat. While concern about growing Soviet military power in areas close to Japan, especially in the disputed Northern Islands, is increasing among the Japanese people, there is little real anxiety that the Russians will actually invade Japan. The Japanese do not fear the Soviet Union enough to support a large defense buildup. This public attitude has come to be reflected in the meager defense budget. The United States perceives the Russian threat to Japan differently and as a result has annual defense expenditures approaching $300 billion. The result has been demands by the Reagan administration that Japan do more to build her defenses. The White House has pressured Japan and a key focus of U.S. interest is the Sea of Japan. The area provides an essential passageway for Soviet warships leaving Vladivostok. To reach the North Pacific, ships must pass Japan through three narrow straits, Tsushima, Tsugaru and La Perouse, known to the Japanese as Soya. Pentagon officials suggest that those "choke points" should not be hard to cutoff, although the fear has been expressed that a blockade of the straits could invite a tactical nuclear strike against Japanese ships or American carrier groups. 1. See Map-1.

U.S. Ambassador to Japan, Mike Mansfield, said in a recent interview that he did not believe there was enough defensive strength in the Western Pacific. There is no immediate threat, he said, but a "potential" one. The very size of the Soviet fleet, coupled with its expansion into new Pacific regions, spells danger by definition. 2.   This has produced a dilemma for Japanese defense policymakers that we noted earlier and aptly described by Professor Gerald Curtis - the Japanese leadership is torn between domestically generated pressures for a conciliatory, cautious leadership style and external pressures for a more positive, higher-risk and active leadership role. 3.

Finally there is the constraint imposed by public opinion that ranges from opposition to support of the status quo, to advocacy of a major defense buildup. A major segment of public opinion comprises the minimalists, over 50% of the population, who favor only the minimum rearmament necessary to satisfy the United States. More supportive of defense efforts are the gradualists to be found mostly in the bureaucracy and in elements of the Liberal Democratic Party; they believe that Japan must step up the pace of rearmament in order to share the defense burden with the United States more equitably and in so doing act in a manner befitting Japan's growing international prestige. At the far right are some individuals I think of as Gaullists, such as Ishihara Shintaro, a well-known novelist and member of the ruling Liberal Democratic Party, and Fukuda Nobuyuki, former president of Tsukuba University, among others, who press for a fully rearmed Japan. While the concept of Gaullism is ambiguous and open to various interpretations, it generally reflects a philosophy of ridding Japan of foreign military forces and of regaining the days when Japan had a powerful military and could use it to extend her influence in Asia. The Gaullist position finds little acceptance amongst the Japanese.

These constraints taken together form a substantial obstacle to a stepped-up defense program.

Map 1
Three Straits-Tsushima, Tsugaru, Soya

Outline of Soviet Naval Activities and Military Aircraft Movements Around Japan

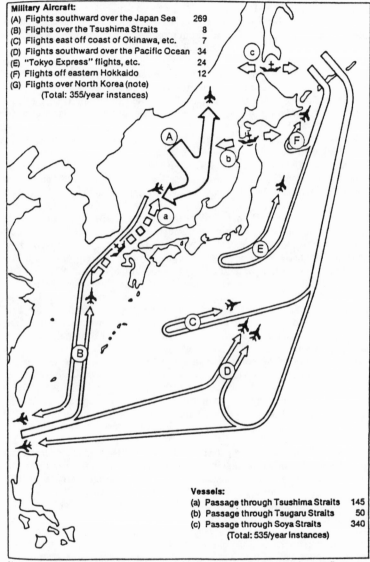

Military Aircraft:
(A) Flights southward over the Japan Sea   269
(B) Flights over the Tsushima Straits   8
(C) Flights east off coast of Okinawa, etc.   7
(D) Flights southward over the Pacific Ocean   34
(E) "Tokyo Express" flights, etc.   24
(F) Flights off eastern Hokkaido   12
(G) Flights over North Korea (note)
     (Total: 355/year instances)

Vessels:
(a) Passage through Tsushima Straits   145
(b) Passage through Tsugaru Straits   50
(c) Passage through Soya Straits   340
     (Total: 535/year instances)

Notes: 1. Number of ships and instances indicates average figures over the past five years.
       2. (G) Flights over North Korea were confirmed for the first time in 1985. Seven flights were made that year.

Source: Defense of Japan, 1986, Japan Defense Agency

Civilian/Military Relations and the Defense Program
Civilian Control

Civilian control was the cornerstone of postwar defense policy in Japan but it was a new concept for the Japanese. Their first inkling of its power came with the firing of General Douglas MacArthur by President Harry Truman on April 11, 1951. John K. Emmerson, the late distinguished diplomat and scholar, described the immediate reaction of Japanese leaders and the mass media as one of shock and dismay. General MacArthur, with his aloofness, arrogance, and his supreme confidence, had filled a vacuum created by the defeat. The Emperor was a figurehead revered by the people, but never considered a leader. The military, which had appropriated power and carried out conquests in China and Southeast Asia, all in the name of a "Holy War," "the New Order in East Asia," and "The Greater East Asia Co-Prosperity Sphere," saw its senior officers and certain civilian leaders tried as war criminals, some executed. MacArthur was the power, both literally and figuratively, and he carried out his responsibilities with majesty and pomp. Comments made after his dismissal suggested Japanese attitudes toward him. The President of the House of Councillors eulogized: "The sudden news was so shocking to me that I have not yet recovered from its effects. " He referred to the "irrevocable loss and bewilderment ... shared by the people of entire Japan. " The two leading newspapers at the time, *Asahi* and *Mainichi,* in a joint editorial. expressed widespread sentiments: "We feel as if we had lost a kind and loving father. His recall is the greatest shock since the end of the war. "

The reactions to Truman's dramatic and sudden action were those of bewilderment and astonishment that an unprepossessing civilian in Washington, even though President, could by one stroke of the pen fire a man who had come to represent to the Japanese people benign Authority and Power. This, it began to dawn on many Japanese, was "civilian control. " The principle became embedded in the new Constitution and in the laws which later created the Self Defense Forces. 4.

It was a principle that U.S. Occupation authorities insisted upon and which was eagerly sought by the Japanese Government in the belief that lack of control of the Imperial Armed Forces had led to adventures in China, a major war, a disastrous defeat and occupation by a foreign army.

However, Japanese civilians had never been responsible for military affairs and had little experience in dealing with the military. Therefore the first solution for establishing civilian control of the military was to bring in police officials and bureaucrats from the old Home Ministry. Their strength was their administrative ability and experience. Their weakness was their ignorance of military affairs.

Another solution, as we noted earlier, was to have selected officials from other government ministries such as Finance, International Trade and Industry, Health and Welfare and Foreign Affairs take charge of procurement, the budget, liaison with foreign countries and military medicine. This was the beginning of the dominance of seconded officials in the Internal Bureaus.

These officials have generally remained in the JDA for only two or three years after which they return to their parent ministries or retire. However, when occupying Internal Bureau positions, their loyalties are seldom questioned and they often aspire to become the Administrative Vice Minister, the highest career position in the JDA, rather than return to their own agency. Several seconded officials have been appointed Administrative Vice Minister, one being Yazaki Shinji, a Finance Ministry official who headed the Defense Policy Bureau before his promotion on June 5,1985. He succeeded Natsume Haruo, a JDA careerist. The latest is Shishikura Muneo who succeeded Yazaki in the spring of 1987 and, like Yazaki, was a former Finance Ministry official. Shishikura formerly held the post of Director General of the Defense Facilities Administrative Agency.

The policy of civilian control of the military establishment has had the steady support of the government and the media, the latter in a rare display of agreement with the government on a defense issue, and firm public backing. Military officers sometimes chafe under these conditions and on occasion voice their frustrations, such as the time General Kurisu Hiroomi complained publicly that the military needed more authority. The Prime Minister promptly fired him.

Historically, the concept of civilian control is rather alien to Japan and this has led some military officers to hold their civilian superiors in low esteem. This is in part due to their belief that civilian control is an aspect of the "abnormal" state of Japanese defense policy since the end of World War II and that an eventual return to normalcy will bring control of military affairs back to the military where they believe it rightfully belongs.

On the other hand, civilian officials are not always considerate toward military personnel. Senior military officers have found it difficult to obtain influential assignments in the Internal Bureaus and this has been a special bone of contention between military and civilian officials. Some efforts have been made to assign selected military officers to the Internal Bureaus but it has had little effect on the primacy of civilian authority. The public's fear of resurgent militarism acts to reinforce civilian dominance of military affairs.

Despite the often contentious bureaucratic tug-of-war that goes on between military officers and civilian officials, a contest often shielded from public view, they do find common ground on defense policy, most notably on the defense budget.

Military and civilian personnel work together in formulating the initial budget and have found that such cooperation facilitates later discussions with the Finance Ministry and members of the LDP. The military side acknowledges the primacy of civilian officials in the budget process and welcomes their support, especially if the concerned officials are seconded from the ministries of Finance or International Trade and Industry. Military officers believe such officials are often in a better position than JDA careerists to obtain results desired by the military services.

As work on the budget proceeds in the JDA, there is constant contact, as noted, between the military service and civilians in the Internal Bureaus. While this goes on, Internal Bureau officials meet informally with their counterparts in the Finance Ministry and MITI at proper bureucratic levels (division chief to division chief; deputy director general to deputy director general, etc.) to obtain a "feel" for what is negotiable.

The continual manuevering among bureaucrats at various levels eventually produces the firm outlines of a defense budget that usually remains intact as the budget moves up the bureaucratic ladder into the political arena. Once the budget reaches this point, there generally is a consensus among concerned politicians and bureaucrats on the percentage increase that will finally be allowed.

The Internal Bureaus are the moving force in much of the *nemawashi* or back-stage manuevering that goes on and it impacts significantly on final budget decisions. I see little change in its ability to influence budget proceedings so long as it can depend on able civilians drawn from the powerful Finance and International Trade and Industry ministries or create a highly capable career service of its own.

There is some sentiment among defense experts that the military services are slowly gaining more influence in defense policy, especially in the budget process, due to their greater in-depth knowledge of special military issues. The responsibility of the military services for the defense of Japan gives them a potentially powerful weapon to gain the essential resources necessary to carry out their missions. Yet, a lack of strong political and bureaucratic support, has stymied their efforts. While some competition for influence on the budget exists between civilian and military personnel, it has so far not surfaced as an issue in the JDA. Civilian officials continue to have the final word within the agency on defense matters.

Career Service

To lessen reliance on other ministry officials, the JDA in the late 1950s began recruiting graduates from the Law Faculties of Tokyo and Kyoto Universities, the traditional source for Japan's bureaucratic elite. Progress has been slow and the number of recruits small. Only about ten career officers are recruited annually for the Internal Bureaus, a factor severely limiting the Internal Bureaus' ability to fill its top positions with career officials. The ministries of Finance, International Trade and Industry and Foreign Affairs appear determined to retain the top jobs in the Internal Bureaus and through skillful and aggressive manuevering they have so far been able to hold on to key posts. A sometimes ally in their efforts are the three military services who want these influential bureaus manned by seconded officials whom they believe to be more experienced, broader in their thinking and better able to obtain sorely needed funds and equipment.

Yet the JDA, encouraged by pro-JDA members of the LDP, especially those in the Policy Affairs Research Council associated with Mihara Asao, an influential Council leader, is trying to strengthen the career service by sending four or five of its brightest career officials to MITI, Finance and the Foreign Ministry to train for two years. When they return, they are assigned to important units in the Defense Policy, Equipment, or Finance Bureaus , or to the Minister's Secretariat. Assignments to these major ministries broaden their vision, deepen their experience and create new friendships which facilitate future cooperation.

The JDA has some distance to travel before its career officers can seriously challenge seconded officials. As the JDA gains stature in the public eye and attracts young aspiring bureaucrats, however, its career service will gain more power and influence in policy councils. Striving for good relations with other government agencies is helping build the career service by exchanging personnel with Finance, MITI, and the Foreign Ministry, and through the publication of its annual White Paper. These actions are building better understanding for JDA objectives and its role in defense policy. In the Japanese bureaucratic world, status and prestige bring their rewards and the JDA works hard to project itself as a key player in the defense establishment. However, the JDA must still contend with hostility from government agencies that are experiencing budget cuts under the government's fiscal austerity program while it continues to enjoy annual increases.

Chapter 3

The National Defense Program Outline (TAIKO)

Origin

As one of the key pillars of Japanese defense policy, the National Defense Program Outline (NDPO) is the charter for the present defense buildup; it sets the parameters for the bureaucrat and politician in deciding on defense matters. It has become institutionalized in the public mind as a deterrent to resurgent militarism and as an expression of the nation's will for peace.

The NDPO was established as official government policy on October 19, 1976. It marked a significant departure from previous defense programs which included one three-year plan (FY 1958-1960) and three successive five-year plans (FY 1962-66, 1967-71, and 1972-76). These plans all stressed the importance of improving the fighting capabilities of the SDF and preparing the military for any eventuality.

In 1972, Prime Minister Tanaka Kakuei set in motion the events which were to culminate in the creation of the NDPO when he directed the JDA to set limits on Japan's peacetime defense forces. After careful consideration by JDA bureaucrats, some general principles on spending and force levels were established but they were inadequate to satisfy growing public pressure for cutbacks in defense spending. From these general discussions, however, came the original idea for the NDPO, "defense power during peacetime", a concept inspired the late Kubo Takuya, who was chief of the Defense Policy Bureau of the JDA from 1970-1974 and Administrative Vice Minister from 1975 to 1976. Central to Kubo's thinking was the belief that it was unnecessary to equate the level of defense preparedness to the threat, as previous defense buildup programs had done. Kubo was convinced that Japan was spending too much on the SDF and that detente and a presumed lessening of tensions between the United States and the Soviet Union provided the right climate to develop a new concept of defense, one emphasizing "defense power in peacetime". Kubo's idea was strongly supported by Sakata Michita, then Director General of the JDA and a former Speaker of the Lower House of the Diet. Sakata believed it necessary to establish a clear limit on defense capability and defense spending so as to attain public consensus on defense matters. He, together with Prime Minister Miki Takeo, exerted strong political leadership in formulating and adopting the NDPO. Along the way, they were opposed by military leaders and followers of the former head of the Defense Bureau in the JDA, Kaihara Osamu. During the formative stages of the NDPO, the then Director General of the JDA, Nakasone Yasuhiro, also opposed Kubo's thinking. Despite this opposition, Miki and Sakata were able to gain sufficient political backing from important faction leaders in the LDP who were increasingly concerned with what they considered an overly ambitious defense buildup program.

The NDPO, with its emphasis on peace, assumed that detente between the United States and the Soviet Union would continue, that the credibility of the U.S.-Japan relationship would not be jeopardized, that Soviet expansionism would be curbed by NATO's military buildup, unrest in Eastern Europe and a

21

poor Soviet economic performance, that there would be no Sino-Soviet reproachment, and that a status quo on the Korean peninsula would be maintained.

Of equal importance were domestic economic and political considerations. Public pressure called for a clear limit on defense spending. Japanese leaders found the NDPO an appealing answer to their financial problems, problems brought on by a shift in the Japanese economy away from high growth and by sharp increases in the price of weapon systems following the oil crisis.

The NDPO was born during detente and its underlying philosophy was to stress the importance of a "peaceful" SDF. It also afforded opportunities to budget managers and power brokers within the government and the LDP to put a brake on defense spending and keep the security issue from becoming too politically controversial.

Principal Feature of the National Defense Program Outline

The NDPO conceptualized a standard defense force capable of coping with limited or small-scale aggression. It deliberately revised downward the buildup targets to be attained. It emphasized the modernization of weapons systems and equipment and the strengthening of the logistic support system but did not change the basic force structure of the SDF. Implicit in NDPO policy was the conviction that the most appropriate defense goal should be the maintenance of a full surveillance capability in peacetime and the ability to cope with limited or small-scale aggression. The policy also foresaw the eventuality that U.S. forces would not be immediately available to defend Japan but assumed that these forces would at some point come to Japan's assistance, although no time frame was mentioned. The NDPO did not have a realistic assessment of the limitations likely to be imposed upon U.S. capabilities to defend Japan.

The NDPO, a watershed in Japanese defense policy, gave defense planners a relatively free hand to interpret what it meant because of its vagueness as a guide to an effective defense buildup. This situation is a sharp departure from the pre-1976 period when defense planning was more rigid and detailed and there was greater correlation between the SDF mission and the resources available to the SDF to carry out that mission.

The National Defense Program Outline began by stating that the broad objective for Japan's military forces was to safeguard Japan's security by forestalling aggression against Japan in cooperation with the United States. The international situation was then analyzed with the main focus on the policies of the Soviet Union and the United States. Because equilibrium existed between the super powers, it was judged unlikely that there would be aggression against Japan.

The basic defense concept was then discussed and covered such items as the prevention of armed invasion, posture of national defense, the posture of the Ground, Maritime, and Air Self Defense Forces, and the basic policy and matters to be taken into consideration in building up defense capabilities.

The NDPO concluded by directing that (1) reasonable standards for personnel recruitment and consideration of measures aimed at securing quality personnel be established. (2) that effective measures be established to maintain and improve defense facilities and harmonize such facilities with surrounding communities, (3) that attention should be directed toward the effective implementation of equipment acquisition programs, with consideration given to swift emergency resupply and acceptable training and educational programs, and (4) that technical research and development systems for the maintenance and improvement of qualitative levels in the military forces be established.

The NDPO also established personnel and equipment goals for the Ground, Air, and Maritime Forces. The full text of the NDPO is in Appendix E.

Consequences of the National Defense Program Outline for an effective defense buildup

The NDPO inadequately provides for the training and equipment of forces to meet emergency military situations. The concept of peacetime defense has hobbled the SDF and hampered the fulfillment of certain military goals. The Maritime Self Defense Forces, for example, are confined to coastal surveillance and defense (mainly against enemy submarines) but their mission does not include transportation of ground forces. Likewise, the mission of the Air Self Defense Forces does not include support of the MSDF, being limited to surveillance and defense of Japanese airspace. ASDF assistance to the Ground Self Defense Forces is confined to interdicting amphibious landings and limited transportation of GSDF personnel. JDA strategy under the NDPO is to expect an attack against the northern island of Hokkaido and this is where a majority of the GSDF is stationed and where conditions are being readied for resistance.

The NDPO also stipulates that the ASDF must have a certain number of planes and the MSDF a certain number of ships by a specified time but there is no allowance for trained pilots, ammunition, fuel, protection of airfields and the provision of modern communication equipment for the three services. The availability of adequate numbers of torpedoes and other weapons that should be a part of the MSDF arsenal has been underestimated. Such lack of readiness reflects the peacetime strategy of the NDPO but does not answer the question, can Japanese military forces actually be used successfully to defend Japan?

Prospects for Change

Despite these shortcomings, it is doubtful that bureaucrats or politicians will initiate serious efforts to change the NDPO. The National Defense Program Outline has been established policy for over nine years and it would be out of character for the Japanese Government to change a major national policy, especially one so controversial, at an early date. Japanese policy has emphasized consistency as a symbol of validity. Significant changes in policy direction are undertaken only on the pretext of positive public support, especially when a policy is in serious dispute.

Lacking public support for a fundamental change in the NDPO, politicians and bureaucrats will probably opt for gradual change. How far and how fast this can take place will depend largely on public opinion. A majority of the public continues to favor maintenance of the status quo. Most observers believe that the political costs to the LDP of initiating major changes in the NDPO would be prohibitive and this is probably why no major faction leader has announced support for such action. The net result is the probability that the NDPO will remain, with all its faults, the primary guide for Japanese defense policy for some time to come.

Chapter 4

The Mid-Term Planning Estimate-MTPE- (CHUGYO)

Purpose

If the National Defense Program Outline is the charter for Japanese defense policy then the MTPE is the instrument which provides an incremental defense buildup plan to fulfill the broad objectives of the NDPO. Until September 18,1985, when the MTPE became official government policy, it was merely an intradepartmental document of the JDA to define the scope and cost of projects for the three military services and a mechanism to inform the government and the Diet of defense buildup plans. It was, in a sense, a "shopping list" for the three military services.

The MTPE, as originally conceived, covered a period of five years from the second fiscal year following the year when the estimate was formulated. It was not a fixed plan like the pre-1976 multi-year buildup programs but was subject to annual review. A new MTPE is prepared every three years.

Work on updating the MTPE usually begins in January when senior officials of the JDA meet to consider recommendations of the three military services for new equipment and improved support activities. To work out basic strategy, initial discussions are held between officials of the Defense Policy Bureau and their counterparts in the GSDF, ASDF, and MSDF. As negotiations proceed and the outlines of military requests become clear, other offices in the Internal Bureaus, mainly Equipment and Finance, join the discussions and preliminary decisions are made on procurement items and budget strategy. These decisions form the basis for the annual JDA budget requests. The most recent MTPE has emphasized the importance of strengthening air defense and anti-submarine activity.

The New MTPE or Five-Year Plan (1986-1990)

Since the MTPE has now become official government policy, speculation has been rife about its effects on defense spending. During much of the summer of 1985, Prime Minister Nakasone worked hard to convince LDP leaders that the 1% of GNP ceiling on defense spending was having a serious impact on the defense buildup and should be removed. His apparent strategy was to make the MTPE official policy while at the same time eliminating the 1% ceiling. After protracted negotiations within the LDP, party leaders and Cabinet ministers decided to accept Nakasone's recommendation that the MTPE become official government policy, but rejected his call for removing the 1% ceiling. Many LDP members apparently felt that dropping the 1% cap while elevating the MTPE to official policy would generate serious opposition, particularly from the Socialist Party, and could lead to a vote of no-confidence. Mr. Nakasone did not want to risk dissolving the Diet by pressing the issue. [The overwhelming victory of the LDP in the July 1986 national elections and the agreement of party leaders that Nakasone could stay on as Prime Minister for another year (his term will now expire in October 1987) virtually assures that the defense program will be strengthened.]

As I will explain in Chapter 6 in more detail, the Cabinet formally scrapped the 1% policy on January 24, 1987, but assured an aroused Opposition and a skeptical public that the government would be prudent in developing the defense budget.

The new five-year plan (1986-1990) revives the pre-1976 fixed five-year formula whereby the contents of a defense buildup plan are detailed and the estimated total expenditures required to implement the program are specified in advance. This is a major departure from the post 1976 MTPE system that required planning on an annual basis.

The new plan sets a guideline for defense spending for the period 1986-1990 at $120 billion at the exchange rate of 150/1, to be spent over a period of five years, ending in March 1991; that is 1.04% of the projected GNP for five years. The new MTPE is to be prepared every three years. Regardless of these guidelines, the defense budget must still be negotiated on an annual basis and there is no assurance that the ultimate spending goal of $76 billion will be met. Defense analysts believe that the new MTPE will probably give the JDA more political influence with LDP leaders and "clout" with the Finance Ministry in negotiating future defense appropriations.

Under the new MTPE, priority will be given to improving air defense capability, modernizing GSDF divisions, attaining a better balance between frontline equipment and logistical support elements, adding new technological innovations to ships of the MSDF and increasing the effectiveness of intelligence gathering, reconnnaissance, command and communication, combat sustainability and readiness. These improvements are mandatory if SDF defense capability is to reach acceptable levels.

Some defense experts worry about the absence of a conceptual framework for these priorities in the new MTPE and whether there is a will on the part of the government and the LDP to provide the necessary resources. A major weakness of the new MTPE, defense analysts contend, is its lack of a concept within which Japanese defense strategy can be formulated in precise terms so that the public can better understand defense policy objectives and the need for increased funds to meet these objectives.

The new plan does clarify how Japan's air defense capability can be strengthened, how the seas surrounding Japan can be safeguarded by improving the effectiveness of the Maritime Self Defense Forces, and what must be done to improve the firepower of the Ground Self Defense Forces. Ways to improve intelligence, reconnaissance and command/communication capabilities are outlined. Combat sustainability, education and training systems, medical care, technology research and development are all addressed. The plan concludes by vowing to be cost-effective. The new MTPE will be reviewed as occasion demands but no later than every three years, at which time military goals will be adjusted based upon economic and financial circumstances, the international situation, and technological trends. A full text of the new plan, translated by the American Embassy, Tokyo, including a chart comparing the goals of the new plan with the objectives of the NDPO will be found in Appendix D.

Planners in the JDA and pro-defense LDP members appear optimistic that a new watershed in Japanese defense policy has been reached with the elevation of the MTPE to a national policy. Even if the NDPO and the MTPE become better understood by the public, there is no assurance that such understanding will translate into greater defense spending. Rather, given the past history of the defense budget process, it appears unlikely that substantial increases will be realized to meet some of the more ambitious goals of defense planners.

26

The *Sankei* newspaper, in an article dated September 19, 1985, complained that the National Defense Program Outline is responsible for the "peacetime" level of defense preparedness. The paper noted that a serious obstacle to maintaining Japanese security will arise if Japan fails to maintain its defense buildup schedule. Adherence to the 1% ceiling is an inflexible policy that cannot adjust to changes in the international situation or to the progress being made in military technology. Even if Japan were to exceed the 1% ceiling by even a small degree, according to the Sankei, there is little danger of Japan becoming a formidable military power.

The *Tokyo Shimbun* of September 19, 1985, expressed guarded optimism about the new MTPE, noting that it lays special emphasis on strengthening forces to defend the skies over the Japanese homeland and guaranteeing the safety of marine transportation. Nevertheless, the article criticized the new Plan for dealing only in vague terms with such important considerations as the introduction of sophisticated radar equipment, Aegis ships equipped with new ship-to-air missile systems, and selection of the successor to the support fighter, F-1. The newspaper cast doubt on the need for 100 P3C anti-submarine patrol aircraft, suggesting that they are being purchased because of American pressure and U.S. complaints over the growing Japanese trade surplus with the United States.

In order to support the objectives of the new MTPE and to gain greater public acceptence and understanding of Japanese defense policy, the Defense Agency has organized a committee called, "Operations Management Autonomous Inspection Committee", headed by Shishikura Muneo, the newly appointed Vice Minister of JDA.

The committee's objectives include producing recommendations for administrative reform of the Self Defense Forces leading to greater unification of command to deal with emergencies, and to provide a conceptual framework for the new MTPE.

The new 5-year plan will undoubtedly attract more skeptics as the JDA attempts to implement its provisions. The crucial test will be how defense budget policy evolves to meet the goals of the new program.

Chapter 5

The Defense Budget Process

The Defense Budget
Major Elements

Spending levels for defense have varied over the years. The defense budget increased 17.7% in 1970, 19.3% in 1972, and 21% in 1975. From 1976, there has been a gradual decline in the rate of increase and it has now leveled off at about 7%. Since 1970, defense spending has been below 1% of the Gross National Product (GNP). (See Tables 1 and 2 for a more detailed breakdown.)

Since the second half of the 1960s, Japan has kept defense expenditures under 1% of GNP. Due to rapid economic expansion in the 1960s and 1970s, annual growth in defense outlays was maintained at a relatively high level for nearly two decades, with an average increase of 12.6% (real terms 7.9%) in the 1960s and 14% (7.8%) in the 1970s. Nevertheless, in comparison with NATO countries which have military expenditures of between 3% and 5% of their GNP, Japan's defense expenditures in absolute terms are small.

Inasmuch as capital spending has been between 20%-25% for the military services, the SDF is restricted to being a lightly equipped military force. Taking the defense budget for 1976 as an example, West Germany spent 42.5% for personnel costs and 32.5% for capital expenditures while Japan spent 56% for personnel costs with 19.6% going for capital outlays.

Money earmarked for direct and indirect maintenance of Japanese and American bases is a distinctive feature of Japan's defense budget. In 1960, money for this kind of support was about 5% of the defense budget but annual increases in the 1970s brought the figure to over 10%. Such expenditures have placed limitations on resource allocations to the three military services.

Defense budget entitlements consume a major part of the budget, personnel costs averaging about 45%, future obligations about 20% and logistical support another 20%. These percentages vary year to year but generally are in these proportions. The remaining 15% is the negotiable part of the budget, the area where the politicians and bureaucrats interact to achieve a consensus and where the ultimate political decisions are made on how much of an increase will be approved and for what purposes.

The 15% sector is the arena where the bureaucrats of the Finance Ministry and JDA civilians and military officers face off in long negotiations over how much of an increase to allow and for what purposes. While these meetings are going on, efforts are made on both sides to enlist the support of influential politicians and key officials in MITI and the Foreign Ministry. Haggling over this part of the budget has become more intense since the imposition of the 1% ceiling in 1976.

A major dilemma for Japanese policymakers in establishing priorities within the 15% limitation, for example, is how to respond to American pressure to expand Japan's responsibilities to include air and sea surveillance up to 1000 miles from Japan and still keep within the guidelines of the National Defense

Table 1
Changes in Japan's Defense Expenditures
1955–1986

Changes in Defense Expenditures (Original Budget)

(Unit: ¥100 million, %)

Item / FY	GNP (initial forecast) (A)	General Account (original) (B)	Growth from Previous Year	Defense Budget (original) (C)	Growth from Previous Year	Ratio of Defense Budget to GNP (C/A)	Ratio of Defense Budget to General Account (C/B)
1955	75,590	9,915	-0.8	1,349	-3.3	1.78	13.61
1965	281,600	36,581	12.4	3,014	9.6	1.07	8.24
1975	1,585,000	212,888	24.5	13,273	21.4	0.84	6.23
1980	2,478,000	425,888	10.3	22,302	6.5	0.90	5.24
1982	2,772,000	496,808	6.2	25,861	7.8	0.93	5.21
1983	2,817,000	503,796	1.4	27,542	6.5	0.98	5.47
1984	2,960,000	506,272	0.5	29,346	6.55	0.99	5.8
1985	3,146,000	524,996	3.7	31,371	6.9	0.997	5.98
1986	3,367,000	540,886	3.0	33,435	6.58	0.993	6.18

Source: Defense of Japan, 1986. Japan Defense Agency

Table 2
Outline of Defense Expenses

Outline of Defense Expenses

Classification	FY 1986	FY 1985
Defense expenses	¥3,343.5 billion	¥3,137.1 billion
% growth from previous year	6.58%	6.9 %
Ratio to GNP	0.993%	0.997%
Ratio to general-account budget	6.18 %	5.98 %
Contract authorization and continuing expenditure	¥1,343.3 billion	¥1,254.9 billion
Future obligation	¥2,418.3 billion	¥2,305.8 billion
(New)	(¥1,321.4 billion)	(¥1,232.8 billion)

Source: Defense of Japan, 1986. Japan Defense Agency

Program Outline (NDPO). (See Map-2).

Some clarification of the issue was given by Richard Armitage, Assistant Secretary of Defense for International Security Affairs, at a meeting of the Pacific and Asian Affairs Council in Honolulu On January 17,1986. He explained that defense of the sea lanes by Japan does not call for stationing destroyers, anti-submarine patrol aircraft or air-to-air interceptors every so many miles between Tokyo and Guam and between Osaka and the Bashi Channel. Although these two approximately 1000-mile routes represent major arteries of Japanese commerce, the best defense, said Mr. Armitage, cannot and should not be reduced to a mechanical formula. The United States has never suggested such a plan to Japan. He further noted that defense to 1000 miles makes no sense for Japan if the United States is not working with Japan inside 1000 miles and is not defending Japan outside 1000 miles.

However, since Mr. Suzuki gave his promise to President Reagan on the 1000 mile issue, JDA, in studying ways in which Japan could fulfill her responsibilities, has run up against the hard realities of an inadequate defense budget. The scenario developed so far is to provide resources for the purchase of aircraft, radar, and other surveillance edquipment, principally for the Maritime and Air Self Defense Forces. Progress has been slow. Defense officials are distressed, leading LDP politicians are unsure how the commitment to the United States can be finally carried out, the Finance Ministry is unsympathetic to JDA budget requests, and the Opposition in the Diet and most of the media are critical.

The apportionment of funds also creates competition and rivalry among the three services. For the past decade, the Maritime and Air Self Defense Forces have received about 40% of the defense budget while the Ground Self Defense Forces received nearly 60%, half of which went for personnel costs. Recently, however, the defense budget procurement allotment has allowed the GSDF only 20% whereas the MSDF and ASDF obtained 80%. This shift in procurement budget priorities reflects in part a developing trend toward support for specific missions of the armed forces rather than merely meeting general procurement goals established by NDPO. Air and sea surveillance to a thousand miles from Japan's shores and greater reliance by the air and maritime forces on modern weapon technology are other factors producing this shift in priorities.

The GSDF has stoutly resisted this budget trend but with little success. Public attitudes toward the Soviet threat and constant pressure from the United States to persuade the SDF to place more emphasis on missions involving the ASDF and MSDF have combined to reduce the percentage of procurement funds for the GSDF.

Resource allocations within the defense budget provide important clues about defense policy priorities. Table 3 confirms that personnel and supply categories have consistently received between 45% and 50% of defense funding and R&D the smallest percentage.

The Budget as a Reflection of National Priorities

A country's national budget tells much about societal priorities. As Japan emerged from defeat and gained her independence in 1952, it was clear that national policy would stress fiscal and monetary programs to rebuild the war-shattered economy and improve the standard of living of Japanese citizens. The budget would provide heavy funding for social services, education and public works and would support those burgeoning industries forming the foundation for Japan's amazing economic recovery.

The results of that national commitment can be seen today as Japan is

Map-2

Defense of Sea Lanes to 1000 miles

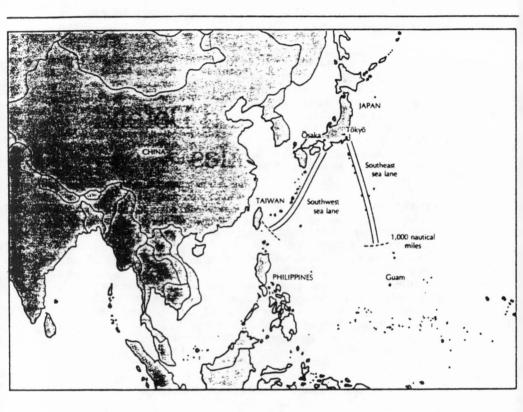

Source: Defense of Japan, 1986

Table 3

Changes in Composition of Defense Expenditures (Original Budget)

(Unit: ¥1 billion, %)

FY / Item	1982 Budget	1982 Distribution rate	1983 Budget	1983 Distribution rate	1984 Budget	1984 Distribution rate	1985 Budget	1985 Distribution rate	1986 Budget	1986 Distribution rate
Personnel; Provisions	1,205.3	46.6	1,225.8	44.5	1,309.4	44.6	1,414.0	45.1	1,508.6	45.1
Supplies	1,380.8	53.4	1,528.4	55.5	1,625.2	55.4	1,723.2	54.9	1,835.0	54.9
Equipment acquisition	580.3	22.4	684.4	24.9	772.5	26.3	822.1	26.2	899.7	26.9
R & D	28.5	1.1	31.4	1.1	36.4	1.2	50.4	1.6	57.7	1.7
Facility improvement	58.6	2.3	53.1	1.9	39.3	1.3	44.2	1.4	56.2	1.7
Maintenance	408.7	15.8	448.4	16.3	454.0	15.5	472.2	15.1	481.5	14.4
Base countermeasures	268.9	10.4	274.7	10.0	285.5	9.7	296.5	9.5	301.1	9.0
Others	35.8	1.4	36.3	1.3	37.5	1.3	37.7	1.2	38.9	1.2
Total	2,586.1	100.0	2,754.2	100.0	2,934.6	100.0	3,137.1	100.0	3,343.5	100.0

Notes: 1. Equipment acquisition expenditures include those for weapons, vehicles, aircraft and vessels.
2. Maintenance expenditures include those for housing, clothing and training.
3. The component ratio of the budget is below 100 percent, because fractions of breakdown figures are rounded.

Source: Defense of Japan, 1986

close to having the second most powerful economy in the world and citizenry esconced in comfortable middle class living.

It is a remarkable record of achievement for a country that turned its back on militarism and devoted its resources to the good life.It probably would not have been possible without a firm national decision to rely on the United States for its security and maintain only a modest defense force. This national resolve meant a defense budget that has proved inadequate to equip the SDF on even a modest scale. (See Table 4.)

Problems in Defense Budget Management - Deferred Payments

A troublesome problem for defense budget managers is the system of deferred payments whereby the JDA postpones or defers payment on equipment purchased for the SDF. The debt owed to defense contractors is climbing annually and is causing the JDA to fall further behind in its efforts to meet the goals of the NDPO and the MTPE and to respond to American pressure for a more equitable sharing of the defense burden. The main fault lies with the policy of capping defense spending at 1% of GNP. To attempt to meet these growing obligations, the Internal Bureaus, military services and Finance Ministry officials annually negotiate the amount to be applied to deferred payments. When agreement is reached, never without a struggle, the figure moves through the budget process without change and becomes the final funding allotment to be applied to the accumulated debt.

Future budgets are already heavily committed to payments for big ticket acquisitions made in previous years. Major defense purchases are thus made on a "buy now, pay later" basis with increasingly alarming results for the defense budget.

In contracting for an aircraft, for example, the JDA will normally spread payments over a four or five year period. If there are insufficient funds in a particular year to pay the defense contractor, the JDA might agree to pay the contractor's loan interest or offer other inducements to alleviate his financial problems. If the JDA cannot make an initial down payment on its contract for an aircraft or a ship, the contractor may have to borrow money from a bank in order to begin production.

Money currently borrowed to pay for modern weapon systems is a burden to be borne in future years. In FY 1984, the JDA "debt" for equipment purchases totalled $6.5 billion at the exchange rate of 150/1 or about 30% of the budget compared to $4.2 billion in FY 1977. In FY 1984, the JDA gave a downpayment of $230 million for the purchase of F-15 fighter planes, P3C anti-submarine patrol planes, escort vessels and other equipment amounting to $6.7 billion. In fiscal 1986, the Defense Agency planned to purchase an A-class guard ship of the Hatsuyuki class for $342 million with a downpayment of only $26 million. The Air Self Defense Forces will buy three CH47 transport helicopters for 38 billion yen with no downpayment. The amount of downpayment for all frontline military equipment has been decreasing year by year. Compared to ten years ago, annual disbursements for military equipment has increased 2.2 times but deferred payments have increased 3.2 times.

The burden of future payments has grown measurably because of the JDA's priority of purchasing frontline (new weapon systems) rather than rear support supplies such as ammunition, fuel and other logistical items. In part, the priority has been set as a result of urgings by the United States to modernize the SDF.

Even though a high priority has been given to defense spending under Prime Minister Nakasone, deferred payments continue to complicate the defense

Table 4
Expenditures in Comparison with
Other Important Budget Items

(Unit: ¥100 million, %)

Item FY	General Account Outlays	Defense Outlays	Composition Ratio	Social Security Outlays	Composition Ratio	Education Science Outlays	Composition Ratio	Expenses related to Public Undertakings	Composition Ratio
1955	9,915	1,349	13.6	1,043	10.5	1,308	13.2	1,635	16.5
1965	36,581	3,014	8.2	5,183	14.2	4,751	13.0	7,333	20.0
1975	212,888	13,273	6.2	39,282	18.5	25,921	12.2	29,120	13.7
1980	425,888	22,302	5.2	82,124	19.3	45,191	10.6	66,554	15.6
1982	496,808	25,861	5.2	90,848	18.3	4,852.5	9.8	66,554	13.4
1983	503,796	27,542	5.5	91,398	18.1	47,970	9.5	66,554	13.2
1984	506,272	29,346	5.8	93,211	18.4	48,323	9.5	65,200	12.9
1985	524,996	31,371	5.98	95,736	18.2	48,409	9.2	63,689	12.1
1986	540,886	33,435	6.2	98,346	18.2	48,445	9.0	62,233	11.5

Note: In this table, figures related to 1980 and thereafter were rearranged on the fiscal 1986 budget basis for the convenience of comparison.

Source: Defense of Japan, 1986. Japan Defense Agency

account. They are an expanding component of the defense budget. Whereas 21% of spending in FY 1978 was for orders made in earlier years, the ratio has now reached 36%. Over the last decade, obligatory outlays have tripled, while total defense spending has not quite doubled.

This has naturally meant holding down spending in other areas of the defense budget. It is difficult, however, to scrimp on items in the personnel and provisions category - pay and food for the Self Defense Forces; nor can the SDF do without fuel for training maneuvers. The result of investing heavily in new weapons systems has been a general deterioration in the living quarters for SDF personnel. Expenditures for this modern equipment was intended to match armament being retired. But no real allowance was made for the abrupt deceleration of the Japanese economy, By the time the 1% ceiling was put in place in 1976, the growth rate for the economy had slipped below 10%, and thereafter it dropped to a low of 2-3%. This economic slowdown taken together with the policy of limiting defense spending to 1% of the Gross National Product and a rising rate of deferred payment have seriously affected the defense buildup program.

A graphic example of how deferred payments pose a danger to the Japanese defense effort can be seen in the statistics in Table 5 (Future Obligations) and Table 6 (Assessment of the amount of Contract Authorization). Table 7 shows Trends in the Composition of the Defense Budget.

Unless the defense budget can provide funds to reduce deferred obligations at a rate faster than at present, the Japanese government will be unable to fulfill the goals of the NDPO and the new five-year plan or meet its commitments to the United States.

Budget Decision-Making
Participants - The Human Factor
Bureaucrats - Some General Observations

Managing security in Japan is essentially a 2-tier process. The first level is purely bureaucratic, where such practical issues as the budget, operational plans, force objectives, establishment of resource priorities and personnel and equipment requirements are considered.

The second tier involves essentially political, economic, cultural and international considerations, the sources of major constraints, as we noted earlier, on security policy. The politician must gauge the importance of these forces as he makes the crucial decisions on defense issues. Defense is a testing ground for Japanese political leadership. For this leadership, as we have noted before, is constantly torn between the reality of an anarchical world and a deeply pacifist public.

The bureaucrat is largely insulated from these pressures. Yet, in dealing with the defense budget, he must take into account the feelings of politicians who mirror these concerns.

Budget managers resort to empiricism in developing the annual defense budget. By leaning on the experiences of the past, the bureaucrat can originate budget recommendations that usually find political support among politicians.

The Japanese bureaucracy is an arena of conflict and competing interests; to survive and protect ones's "turf" requires skill, nerve, and patience. The most skillful practitioner of this bureaucratic art is the division chief. He is at the center of the decision-making process and wields considerable influence in the formulation of the defense budget. The power of the division chief derives mainly from knowledge of his area of responsibility and his near monopoly on information. He originates policy recommendations and guides the decision-

Table 5
Future Obligations

| | Outlay | | (Unit: ¥ 1 billion) |
	Total	Equipment	Future Obligation *
1979	¥-2095 bn	¥ 393 bn	¥ 919 bn
1980	2230	461	1272
1981	2400	540	1349
1982	2586	580	1747
1983	2754	684	1975

Table 6
Amount of Contract Authorization

	Request (A)	Budget (B)	(Unit: ¥ 1 billion B/A
1979	¥ 1277 bn	¥ 919 bn	72%
1980	1521	1272	83.6
1981	1579	1349	85.4
1982	2259	1747	77.3
1983	2480	1975	80%

*These figures include future obligations for defense facilities improvement and others, as well as equipment.

Source: These tables were prepared for the author by the Japan Defense Agency, June 2, 1986

Table 7

Trends in the Composition of the Defense Budget

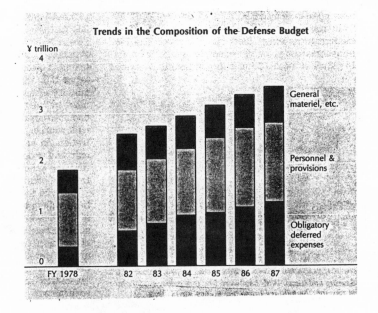

Trends in the Composition of the Defense Budget

¥ trillion

General materiel, etc.

Personnel & provisions

Obligatory deferred expenses

FY 1978   82   83   84   85   86   87

Source: Japan Echo, Volume XIV, Number 2, Summer 1987

making process as it moves both horizontally and vertically.

He is responsible for all the work of his division. He decides what clearances are needed for a particular policy recommendation; he negotiates with division chiefs in other government agencies on defense policy issues, and he and the career officers under his supervision are the only ones empowered by regulation, tradition and custom to issue orders in the division.

In formulating policy for the defense buildup, the division chiefs in the Internal Bureaus and in the three military services work together to produce budget recommendations that can generally survive bureaucratic scrutiny. The durability of the division chief's recommendations is mainly attributable to the time-honored bureaucratic principle of *ringisei* or consensus building. In developing policy recommendations for the defense budget that can gain acceptance in the top echelons of the JDA bureaucracy and the National Defense Council, the division chief must negotiate and compromise differences among rival bureaucracies in order to give each unit in the process a stake in the eventual outcome. A decision having the imprint of consensus can move swiftly through concerned offices and a final decision can be reached in a relatively short time.

While many hours are spent reconciling differences in the consensus process, it insures that all concerned parties have had a voice in the decision-making process and that implementation of the budget will be swift and relatively uncomplicated.

Given Japan's bureaucratic structure, history and traditions, the role of the bureaucrat and politician in defense policy will very likely remain virtually unchanged. Each has staked out his own area of jurisdiction; each has a certain expertise to bring to budget formulation; each has developed the knowledge and ability to negotiate, to compromise and to rationalize policy; and each has his own conception of the national interest and what is the best defense policy for Japan.

As Japan's defense commitments grow and as realization of the need for greater equity in the United States-Japan security alliance deepens, possible shifts in the power relationship among JDA, the Ministry of Finance and MITI bureaucrats may occur. Such shifts could result from growing pressure from the United States, from the continued strong leadership of Prime Minister Nakasone and his successor in defense policy, from a less severe financial situation, from a strengthened career service in the JDA or from unforeseen international developments.

The Politician and the Political Equation

While the role of the bureaucrat in defense policy remains essentially where it has been since the end of World War II, the politician has become more influential. Much of this influence is the result of the LDP's political responsibility to keep United States-Japan relations in equilibrium, especially the security relationship. When American pressure increases for a more effective defense buildup, the politician responds by making the key budget decisions to keep the alliance on course. The bureaucrat often defers to the politician when a defense issue becomes heavily political.

The public's recognition of the importance of the United States-Japan relationship and its support of only a minimal defense buildup effort have created conditions in which military issues are treated as an extension of United States-Japan political relations. American pressures are fed into the Japanese political system where concessions are extracted from politicians in order to preserve the political relationship. This set of circumstances, while leaving a residue of bitterness and dissatisfaction on both sides, has paradoxically enhanced the role of the politician in the defense decision-making process.

As I noted earlier, there are strong political currents in the LDP affecting Japan's defense policy. Because of the still controversial nature of the security issue in Japanese politics (public opinion polls consistently reveal opposition to an ambitious defense program), most politicians in the LDP are reluctant to take a firm public position on defense questions.

Yet political voices are beginning to be heard within the ruling party for a more forthright stand on the defense issue. The leader in this effort is Prime Minister Nakasone, probably the most pro-military of all post-war prime ministers. Many of the pro-defense politicians that are influencing defense policy belong to the so-called Mihara group in the LDP. I mentioned before that Mihara Asao has long advocated a strong defense posture for Japan. He has been joined in this resolve by a nucleus of senior politicians who were formerly Directors General of the Defense Agency such as Kanemaru, Kurihara, Yamashita, Omura, and Ito, among others, and some of Mihara's own proteges such as Shiina Motoo, a brilliant thinker and international strategist for the LDP. Mr. Shiina is presently the chief of the International Bureau of the LDP, has no factional affiliation, and is the son of the former Foreign Minister and Vice President of the LDP, Shiina Etsusaburo.

It is to these politicians that bureaucrats on either side of the defense issue come for support. For example, during the defense budget debate, a high official of the Defense Agency might visit a pro-defense politician to plead his case for more funds for a new communication system, a frigate, an air defense missile, or a stronger tank for the Ground Self-Defense Force. The politician, if convinced of the merits of the JDA case, might consult with like-minded colleagues to gather suppport for the JDA request. This might take the form of informal discussions with more senior members of the LDP to gain the critical support for the JDA case that only the more prestigious leaders of the LDP could provide.

The same politician might also receive a visit from a member of the Budget Bureau of the Finance Ministry who would argue that the JDA was asking for too much and could not justify a request for new frontline equipment in light of austere budget conditions.

During the annual debate on the defense budget, informal discussions between politicians and bureaucrats are constantly in progress with pro and anti forces endeavoring to seek the advantage.

The new Patriot air defense missile is an example of how bureaucrats and politicians interact in working out solutions to procurement problems. When the proposal for the Patriot was first introduced, the GSDF insisted that it have control over the operation of the missile. The ASDF countered that the air force should have management of the missile as it was intended to protect Japanese military airfields. Lobbying was intense on both sides with representatives from the ASDF, GSDF, the Internal Bureaus, MITI and other concerned officials using their links with friendly politicians to gain support for their cause. After months of debate and informal discussions in restaurants, offices, hotels, and private homes, a gradual consensus began to emerge that favored the ASDF as the principal manager of the new Patriot. The ultimate decision involved politicians and bureaucrats and demonstrated the unique value of negotiation and consensus in the Japanese decision-making process.

Politicians and bureaucrats not only interact to shape the defense budget, but they are involved in issues relating to the presence of U.S. forces in Japan. One of the biggest problems, for example, facing Japanese officials is how to maintain the smooth operation of U.S. Forces in Japan. One such issue is securing landing practice grounds for U.S. carrier-based aircraft. The United States has repeatedly urged Japan at various bureaucratic levels to find a suitable site for carrier aircraft to practice night landings. At the Japan-United States summit meeting in January 1985, President Reagan raised the subject with Mr. Nakasone and the Prime Minister promised to find a solution. Landing practice is presently carried out at Atsugi, Misawa, and Iwakuni air bases. The naval air facility at Atsugi, where most of the necessary training takes place, is surrounded by densely populated residential districts. The effect of aircraft noise on the Atsugi residents has created intense opposition to practice landings and local officials are demanding that such landings be discontinued.

The Japanese Government, therefore, decided to ask the residents of Miyake Island located about 100 miles south of Tokyo for permission to build a landing strip for U.S. carrier-based aircraft. Residence of Miyake objected, recalled the mayor and city councilmen favoring the project, and remain adamantly opposed. The Defense Facilities Administrative Agency (DFAA), a part of the Defense Agency, has tried to persuade Miyake islanders to agree to the airfield and has talked to Diet members who represent the island to enlist their support. Pro-defense LDP members have also used their influence with local politicians as well as businessmen and fishing interests but the citizens of Miyake remain unalterably opposed. The process of negotiation and consensus has some distance to travel before a solution to the problem can be found.

Another issue that demonstrates how a consensus is built on an issue involving U.S. Forces in Japan is the case of the visit of the first nuclear-powered submarine, Sea Dragon (SSN), to the port of Sasebo, Japan on November 12, 1964.

Negotiations over the visit between the United States and Japan and within the Japanese Goverenment took 18 months and involved LDP members representing Sasebo and pro-defense Diet members, local officials, the Mayor of Sasebo, fishing interests, DFAA officials, Foreign Ministry personnel and officers of the American Embassy, Tokyo. After all concerned interests had been heard and safety and other questions resolved, the Japanese Goverenment informed the United States that the Sea Dragon's visit could take place. It was a classic example of how bureaucrats and politicians, working together, were able to satisfy the concerns of local residence, fishermen, and anti-nuclear forces that the Sea Dragon posed no danger to Japanese interests. The author represented the American Embassy during the long negotiations with the Foreign Ministry and personally observed the negotiation and consensus procesess in action. It was impressive and highly successful. Since the Sea Dragon's visit, subsequent visits by SSN submarines have gone practically unnoticed. 1.

Internal Bureaus (naikyoku)

Career professionals in the Internal Bureaus formulate and give direction to defense policy. The power alignment in these bureaus depends on many complex factors. Among the most important is the presence or absence of strong leadership in the Defense Policy, Finance, and Equipment bureaus. Competition among these bureaus often reflects the rivalry that exists among the ministries of Finance, International Trade and Industry and the JDA in defense policy. Forceful leadership in these bureaus can give direction and purpose to defense policy and strengthen the position of the JDA in inter-agency negotiations over the defense budget.

In the Internal Bureaus, there are still battles to be fought and won, bureaucratic adversaries to win over and conciliate and political support to be

41

sought. The professional staff in the Internal Bureaus is beginning to make inroads into the entrenched power of the Finance Ministry in the annual struggle over the budget, largely reflecting persistent U.S. pressure for a greater Japanese defense contribution.

Yet experts appear to have mixed feelings about the future of the Internal Bureaus as a primary force in the battle of the budget. Some feel that the quality of personnel continues to be mediocre and that there are too few civilians to deal effectively with a military force numbering over 200,000. Others doubt the ability of the Internal Bureaus to develop a new charter for the SDF to assure continued growth and military effectiveness.

Career officials in the Internal Bureaus, while savoring their leadership positions, still privately smart over the privileged position given "outsiders" as chiefs of the Defense Policy, Finance and Equipment bureaus. I have not observed instances where the career principle has taken firm hold, so that top positions will soon be filled by JDA careerists. On the other hand, the presence of seconded officials adds to the power of the Internal Bureaus in the defense budget debate. Their influence within their own agencies, their knowledge of the JDA and the SDF, their broad vision, bureaucratic experience, finesse in dealing with politicians, and loyalty when assigned to the JDA are all sources of strength for this sometimes embattled agency.

Military Services

Existing in a societal atmosphere of deep and pervasive pacifism, of a Constitution that renounces war as an instrument of national policy, and of firm civilian control of the military, the SDF is seeking to chart a course that will increase its capability to defend Japan. It is not an enviable position for the three military services. A further complication is the lack of an influential constituency in the private and public sectors to support SDF requests for resources to strengthen its capabilities. From the Chiefs of Staff to the privates, there is a sense of frustration over the lack of progress in building an effective military force. Despite these obstacles and strong service rivalry for scarce funds, the SDF appears determined to carry out its mission and to achieve the level of readiness called for in the NDPO and the MTPE.

The military services recognize that they must cooperate with the Internal Bureaus and other civilian officials and politicians to obtain necessary funds and public support. So in the best tradition of the Japanese bureaucracy, they protect their turf yet work toward a consensus.

The three services, because of their close association with personnel of U.S. Forces, Japan(USFJ), often lobby for equipment to strengthen SDF capabilities with key officers in USFJ. These efforts usually gain them valuable allies. The results can be pressures exerted from the American side to acquire new weapons systems for the SDF.

Ministries - Finance, International Trade and Industry, Foreign Affairs

The Finance Ministry has a powerful voice in defense policy because of its control over the national budget. It sets spending levels in the JDA budget that are not easily changed. The only significant leverage available to the JDA for adjustments in these levels is to call on sympathetic Diet members for support.

The key unit in the Finance Ministry dealing with the JDA is the Budget Bureau's JDA division, staffed by career professionals and specialists who are expert on various facets of the JDA budget. Many have served in the Budget Bureau six to eight years and have gained considerable experience and understanding of the defense budget process.

42

The division has separate units that deal with the GSDF, ASDF, MSDF and the Internal Bureaus, and officials in these units are very knowledgeable about budget strategy and tactics of the three military services and the Internal Bureaus. Division experts analyze the relationship of equipment procurement to operational plans and the fulfillment of the NDPO and the MTPE objectives. These officers, hard to fool, are especially adept at deciphering what is bluff in JDA budget tactics.

The JDA budget division in the Finance Ministry begins its study of projected funding requirements for the military in late spring and is prepared for a thorough analysis of the JDA budget when it arrives in August. The division prepares its own budget after detailed discussions with the three military services and the Internal Bureaus. According to one Finance Ministry official, the division, in fashioning its own budget, weighs carefully Japanese commitments under the United States-Japan Security Treaty and other defense arrangements between the two countries and tries to establish priorities consistent with available funds.

The division's responsibility is to balance the needs of the three military services in satisfying major defense goals. Negotiation and compromise are the main ways in which budget decisions are reached. The division wants to appear reasonable, yet its actions in reducing JDA requests are resented by the military services and the Internal Bureaus, the latter often provoked into raising the issue to the political level.

The Ministry of International Trade and Industry has an important voice in defense policy and enters budget negotiations with the JDA when the military services and the Internal Bureaus are considering the type and quantity of military equipment to be purchased. The Equipment Bureau is the principal contact point for MITI and, as I have noted, the head of the bureau is a career MITI official. The Ministry's links with the defense industry and with foreign suppliers give it a unique role in procurement planning to meet military goals.

The Foreign Ministry's role in defense policy and JDA budget preparation is secondary yet indispensable. It establishes the atmosphere for negotiation and for interpreting American attitudes on Japanese security issues. The Foreign Ministry projects an image of neutrality in the budget battle. It also has the advantage of being considered very knowledgeable on broad foreign policy issues and on how Japanese defense policy fits this framework. It often sides with the JDA in budget negotiations because of its stance that a credible defense force is an important part of foreign policy.

Finally, politicians look to the Foreign Ministry for an evaluation of American intentions with regard to United States-Japan security relations. The ministry is often a conduit for conveying American requests for a greater Japanese defense effort, setting the stage for a replay of the dilemma, noted earlier, that face defense policymakers.

Foreign Ministry officials thus exert influence on defense policy in a quiet, unobtrusive way yet with important consequences for negotiations over the defense budget. Their influence remains largely unnoticed by the public but it reverberates in the halls of the Finance Ministry, the JDA, and the Diet.

Budget Strategy
JDA and the Finance Ministry

These two adversaries in the defense budget process generally limit their negotiations to 15% of the budget, that which involves procurement of weapon systems. As noted before, the 85% contains fixed costs including personnel and maintenance expenses and obligations incurred in previous years for weapons procurement. The Finance Ministry has little control over these fixed obligations, so the center of the budget struggle shifts to the 15% residue. There the JDA stakes out its position for increases in "frontline" equipment (new ships, aircraft, tanks, communication and early warning systems, etc.) and augmentation of stockpiles of ammunition, fuel and other support equipment.

Another aspect of JDA-Finance Ministry budget strategy is the imposition on the JDA by the Finance Ministry of what professionals call the "hard budget" system. This is a control device to limit JDA budget flexibility through restriction on transfer of funds from one project to another without ministry approval. It usually takes lengthy negotiations to get such approval.

Although budget negotiations between the JDA and the Finance Ministry outwardly convey the impression of being free-wheeling and tough, they nevertheless comply with traditional Japanese bureaucratic behavior which seeks consensus and avoids open confrontation. Division chiefs in the Internal Bureaus and in the budget bureau of the ministry carry the main burden of negotiations. In the end, these officials usually compromise on an increase in the defense budget that is a guide for politicians in arriving at a final percentage increase.

JDA officials are not timid about using urgent U.S. requests for a greater Japanese defense effort to pressure the Finance Ministry to provide more funds. For example, when Prime Minister Suzuki Zenko suggested to President Reagan that Japan would monitor the sealanes to 1000 miles of Japan, the JDA responded by proposing the acquisition of additional patrol aircraft and naval vessels to accomplish the surveillance mission. The ministry was not persuaded, and made substantial cutbacks in the JDA's FY 1985 budget request. Table 8 provides statistics on JDA budget requests over a six year period, what the Finance Ministry allowed (assessment) and the final budget figure.

The Invisible hand of the Foreign Ministry

As we have just seen, the ministry can be an important factor in Japanese security deliberations. Devices available to influence defense policy are numerous and subtle. For example, the Foreign Minister's friendship with the Finance Minister and his good relations with key officials in the Finance Ministry provide an opportunity for him to sway the thinking of these officials. Key division chiefs and bureau directors general also have several ways of getting their defense views across by contacting important politicians, the Foreign Minister, and the senior ministry official assigned to the Internal Bureaus.

Another method to sharpen the Prime Minister's perception of the budget problem is through private briefings. One of the personal secretaries to the Prime Minister is a Foreign Office official often in a position to brief the Prime Minister on American attitudes toward Japanese defense policy.

A third avenue of influence is the regularly scheduled briefing of the Prime Minister by the Vice Minister of the Foreign Ministry, the ministry's top career official, which occurs every other week. Before this meeting, the Prime Minister usually talks to the American Ambassador to gain a clearer insight about American attitudes toward Japanese defense policy.

The LDP - More Political Influence at Work

Defense policy is becoming more central to United States-Japan relations, and the LDP is thus playing an increasingly significant role in establishing guidelines for the defense budget. The political metamorphosis taking place in the Diet on the security issue is due not only to growing public acceptance of the SDF and concern over Soviet military activity on Japan's doorstep, but to a recognition by Japan's leaders thaed file13d t more needs to be done to build Japan's defenses if security is to be safeguarded and ties to the United States

Table 8
Process of Defense Budget Making

(Unit: ¥ 1 billion)

	Request	Assessment	Addition	Budget
1979	¥ 2134 bn * (12.3% +)	¥ 2065 bn (8.6% +)	30	¥ 2094 bn (10.2% +)
1980	2298 (9.6)	2219 (5.95)	11	2230 (6.48)
1981	2447 (9.7)	2377 (6.6)	23	2400 (7.61)
1982	2580 (7.5)	2555 (6.46)	31	2586 (7.75)
1983	2776 (7.3)	2718 (5.11)	36	2754 (6.5)
1984	2944 (6.88)	2896 (5.15)	39	2935 (6.55)

* ( ) indicates growth rate

Source: This table was prepared for the author by the Japan Defense
Agency, June 2, 1986

strengthened. You could observe this trend in the Diet's Lower House Budget Committee. Here both the LDP and the Opposition debate the defense issue, summon bureaucrats to testify in order to gain an understanding of the direction the defense effort should go.

During these budget sessions, senior officials of the Foreign Ministry, Finance Ministry, MITI, and JDA are on call to testify on particular features of the defense appropriation. For those unlucky enough to have offices far from the Diet building, cots are provided in the Diet so they can be available at the urgent call of the Budget Committee.

Not only the Budget Committee but defense-related committees of the LDP discussed in Chapter 1, figure in the development of defense policy. However, standing committees of the Diet, such as the Budget Committee, wield more influence as they represent all political segments of the Diet whereas most of the committees referred to in Chapter 1, are merely units of the LDP. Yet these latter committees can influence the course of the defense debate because their members can also belong to important standing (permament) committees of the Diet.

Both the LDP and opposition parties carefully guage the public mood and take positions on the defense issue that they believe will bring the most political rewards and the least political pain. Choices are often limited, and the narrower the choice the greater the dilemma facing Japan's politicians.

The 1% issue (to be discussed in Chapter 6) is a case in point. Defense-oriented LDP members led by Prime Minister Nakasone are attempting to obtain more funds for the JDA by proposing the elimination of the 1% ceiling on defense spending. These LDP politicians actively support JDA policies and reject Finance Ministry arguments that Japan cannot afford to spend more for its security.

Yet, faction leaders in the LDP, especially Miyazawa, Abe, and top politicians in the Tanaka faction, together with influential Cabinet members, continue to be cautious on the defense issue and reluctant to underwrite the policies of the pro-defense group. Despite their misgivings, party leaders appear to be moving slowly toward a position of greater defense spending even while paying lip service to the policy of not allowing such spending to exceed 1% of GNP.

Most defense experts believe that the 1% problem is fast becoming a dead issue in defense policy, although the Opposition has not yet given up. Even though LDP leaders and Cabinet ministers accept the need for larger defense appropriations (mostly in private discussions), they realize that the LDP cannot get ahead of public opinion on the defense issue without risking public censure. Yet these same leaders are under direct and indirect pressure from the United States to assume more of the burden for Japan's defense. The dilemma will not go away.

One influential LDP member told me that for a politician to be effective on defense matters, he must have a broad view of the financial problems facing Japan; must have considerable knowledge of international relations and foreign influences on Japanese security policy; and must be trusted by the LDP leadership. The ranks of such politicians, he thought, were growing, as was the defense consciousness of the public. He suggested that by observing the reaction of the Socialist Party on defense issues, especially on the budget, one could gain a better perspective on the changes occurring in public opinion toward Japanese defense policy.

The Opposition

The Opposition (Socialist Party, Komeito, Democratic Socialists and the Communist Party) has put together a rather shaky coalition to oppose one aspect of defense policy, removal of the 1% ceiling on defense spending. The Socialist Party, in particular, has been a strong supporter of the 1% ceiling, not adverse to boycotting budget committee sessions to focus public attention on the issue and to pressure the LDP to retain the cap on defense spending. The boycott tactic often persuades LDP leaders to discuss defense issues, produces ambivalent statements by the Prime Minister on defense policy and particularly defense spending, and achieves a compromise that usually brings the Socialists back to the Budget Committee. The compromise is often an amalgam of fuzzy statements by government leaders on defense policy (Japan will not become a military power but does need a military force capable of defending the country), media pressure to resume Diet proceedings, and an "understanding" among Opposition and LDP leaders on defense policy.

Because of the stunning defeat of the Socialist Party in the July 1986 national election (the party's representation in the Diet dropped from 112 seats to 85 and other opposition parties also lost seats, except the Communists), the Opposition will be less effective in opposing the LDP on defense issues.

All opposition parties accept the existence of the SDF (even the Communists find it difficult to continue to claim that the SDF is unconstitutional), although with varying degrees of enthusiasm. There also appears to be some softening on broader issues of defense policy. For example, when the JDA issued its 1984 White Paper – The Defense of Japan – in which it suggested that Japanese defense forces should be incorporated into the global strategy of the Western nations, it drew some criticism from the major opposition parties although not the shrill censure that has often followed previous JDA policy statements. Even the Democratic Socialist Party noted that it was entirely appropriate for Japan to shoulder its fair share of the defense burden in the Free World.

The Opposition, while privately acknowledging the futility of trying to maintain a lid on defense spending, continues to criticize the government for attempting to expedite the goals of the NDPO. While the Opposition recognizes the inevitability of higher defense costs, the parties are reluctant to agree to remove the cap on defense spending, arguing that to do so would lead to unrestrained military budget excesses.

One newspaper reporter who has studied the defense issue in Japan for many years told me that 60% of Socialist Party members support the SDF. He went on to say that the party has two faces on the defense issue, one public and one private. The deep ideological split in the party is one reason for divided support for the SDF. Viewed in historical perspective, present Opposition policy, especially that of the Socialists, represents a substantial change in attitude, from strident criticism to grudging acceptance.

Chapter 6

The 1% Issue

Raison d'Etre

Placing a ceiling on defense expenditures of 1% of the Gross National product was instituted in 1976 while Miki Takeo was Prime Minister and Sakata Michita, the former Speaker of the Lower House of the Diet, was Director General of the Defense Agency. It came into being at the same time as the National Defense Program Outline and reflected a public mood for tighter restrictions on a defense budget that had increased 17.7% in 1970 to 21% in 1975.

Both policies were also seen as a natural consequence of the high tide of detente and of renewed hope for a peaceful world. Japanese defense policy was to have a new look. It was time to re-direct defense planning, set definitive targets for the defense buildup, redress the imbalance between the fighting units and rear support capabilities, establish spending limits for the JDA and above all gain greater public understanding and support for the SDF. These factors, buttressed by a general belief that a Soviet invasion of Japan was unlikely, were largely responsible for the 1% policy.

On November 5, 1976, when the Miki Cabinet adopted a policy to key defense expenditures to a fixed percentage of the GNP, a figure of 1% found general support among the public, bureaucrats and politicians. For those who wanted increased defense spending, moderate growth in the economy promised more funds for defense. For those who opposed a stepped-up defense effort, the 1% ceiling removed the worry of a possible rapid and massive rearmament.

As long as the economy expanded at a rate of five or six percent, the JDA had few complaints. However, as GNP growth began to slow and NDPO goals were deferred because of lack of funds, the JDA grew increasingly concerned and pressures began to build for a change of policy. However, advocates of change faced the hard reality of a 1% policy that had taken on a life of its own, institutionalized in the public mind as the way to curtail defense spending and check the military.

As the economy grew sluggish and the government was forced to introduce a fiscal austerity program under Prime Minister Suzuki, the Finance Ministry became the principal adversary of JDA, cutting defense budget requests in the name of frugality. The 1% issue thus took on strong political overtones.

Impact on the Defense Budget and Military Capability

The 1% policy has had a profound effect on the ability of the SDF to meet the goals of the NDPO and the MTPE. Bureaucrats and politicians concerned with the defense budget process are aware of its pernicious influence. An irony of the defense budget is that when the 1% ceiling was established, it helped the JDA to secure more funds from the Ministry of Finance. Without the 1% benchmark, the Ministry could theoretically have reduced the defense budget to .06 or .07 of GNP. That this did not happen was considered by defense experts as a salutary consequence of the 1% policy.

As time passed and Japan's fiscal problems worsened, the 1% policy entered a new and worrisome phase. Weapon procurement had to be delayed, buildup goals had to be adjusted and timetables had to be changed. On May 12,1984, the Japanese government conceded that it would not be able to meet its timetable for the defense buildup program and consequently had to approve a three year delay, pushing back completion until early 1991 when weapons programmed to be acquired and in operation by 1988 would merely be acquired.

Each service has felt the brunt of the 1% policy. Since the 1960s, the ratio of expenditures for equipment procurement, facility improvement and maintenance for the GSDF has been declining. This trend became especially conspicuous in 1976 after the establishment of the 1% ceiling. In recent years it has been possible to replace equipment at an annual rate of only 5%. If this continues, it will take nearly 20 years to re-equip the GSDF alone. Putting it another way, the defense equipment of the GSDF is two generations old. In modern warfare, arms this old are virtually useless.

MSDF vessels are weak in electronic warfare capability and in the use of anti-air and anti-ship missles. Most of the torpedoes and mines are obsolete.

The ASDF was supposed to receive 27 sets of short range surface-to-air missles over 5 years but by 1984 it had received only 4 sets.

Military spending has failed to meet the goals of the NDPO or the pledges of recent Prime Ministers to protect sea lanes up to 1000 miles from Japanese shores. Almost from the inauguration of the NDPO, the government began to fall behind. By 1984, 40% of weapons purchased were to have been made under NDPO guidelines but actually only 27% were acquired.

This gloomy analysis of SDF defense capabilities is a reminder of the serious impact the 1% ceiling policy has had on Japanese defense efforts. The Japanese Government now seems to be coming to grips with this reality. Under Prime Minister Nakasone, pressures have been building to obtain more funds for the SDF. American exhortations are helping but the Prime Minister must convince the public that removal of the 1% ceiling is in Japan's own national interest, not being done merely to satisfy the United States. He is thus caught in the traditional defense dilemma.

Prospects for Change

The 1% ceiling policy will be less influential in the future than in the past, having, in a sense, been superceded by the new 5-year defense buildup plan. However it still carries potent symbolic value as a deterrent to excessive military spending and it will have to be repealed before some of its negative features can be overcome.

Most defense experts agree that the policy serves no useful purpose and should be eliminated, especially at a time of growing Soviet military power in Northeast Asia. Many Japanese and American officials contend there would be no 1% ceiling question if Japan merely calculated its defense expenditures as the United States and NATO countries do, namely by including military annuities and pensions in the budget. If such were done, Japanese defense spending would be about 1.6% of GNP. However, for political reasons, these pensions and annuities are included in the Health and Welfare Ministry budget.

More than one defense observer has told me that the percentage of defense spending to GNP will exceed the current 1% ceiling in 1986/87. The cost of frontline weapons currently planned for purchase under the new 5-year buildup plan - 75 F-15 fighter planes, 50 P-30 anti-submarine patrol aircraft, 373 Type 74 tanks, 43 AHIS anti-tank helicopter and 14 destroyers, among other equipment, is becoming increasingly expensive. Under current projections for economic growth, the $76 billion to be spent over a 5 year period under the new plan represents a figure slightly over 1% of GNP.

Prime Minister Nakasone has reiterated the statements of his predecessors that he would abide by the 1% limit. Should Japan carryout the buildup plans envisaged in the NDPO and the MTPE, it would be difficult if not impossible to keep within the 1% ceiling. So far, financial stringencies have limited defense spending, much to the continuing displeasure of American officials.

The criticism of Japan's "inadequate" defense outlays has come loudly from the United States for years. The intensity has increased in parallel with the growing trade deficit. While it is shortsighted to link trade and defense, such linkage has become inevitable as Japan's trade surplus with the United States continues to grow along with the U.S. defense budget. Since the invasion of Afghanistan and the growing alarm in the United States over the rapidity and extent of the Soviet military buildup in East Asia, voices have become more strident in urging Japan "to do more" in sharing the defense burden. The Japanese have retorted that their defense budget "sticks out" among other items, including education and welfare; that their defense budget is the eighth largest in the world, in absolute figures; that their Self Defense Forces are obtaining some of the most sophisticated weaponry in the world; that the public's attitude toward defense has become more supportive; and that the gradual increase planned for the future is not unworthy of a Japan with deep financial troubles and a populace which has had to be educated over a long period of time in the necessity for a self-defense system.

Congressional attitudes have nevertheless been severely critical of Japan, more because of the unemployment figures in industrial cities - some of which are attributed to Japanese competition, especially in automobiles - but also because of the popularly accepted conviction that Japan is not "bearing its weight" in international affairs, especially defense. Several resolutions have been introduced in Congress calling on Japan to increase its security contribution. The latest was a measure approved by voice vote in the House of Representatives on June 18, 1987 requiring Secretary of State George Shultz to enter into talks with Japan to increase Japanese defense spending to at least 3% of GNP.

Prime Minister Nakasone, though supporting the 1% ceiling in principle, has stated that this limit was an artificial figure and that the standard must rather be what is needed for Japan's defense. During 1985 and 1986, the Prime Minister voiced his concern on many occasions that the 1% cap on defense spending was an obstacle to Japan's defense buildup and should be removed. He was finally able to convince the leaders of the LDP, and on January 24, 1987, the Cabinet formally decided to scrap the 1% policy, but hastily assured the public that defense spending would remain "in the area of 1%".

It was a difficult decision for Mr. Nakasone as the 1% policy had become a symbol of Japan's dedication to the spirit of Article 9 of the Constitution. Some political analysts suggested that the leaders of the LDP had for sometime recognized the need to change the 1% policy but had not wanted to take the political risks involved. They were more comfortable with Mr. Nakasone being "out front" on the issue. These analysts also noted that the LDP spectacular election victory in July 1986 gave Mr. Nakasone and his colleagues the confidence to take on the stubborn problem of "1%" with the expectation that the political fallout could be contained.

Nevertheless, the sudden abandonment of a policy that had seemed sacrosanct startled many Japanesea and had immediate political consequences, touching off anti-Nakasone attacks from the major opposition parties. They were shortlived, being overshadowed by the tax controversy.

Despite the predictable harsh reaction of the opposition, no government or LDP leader has suggested that removal of the 1% ceiling means that Japan would stray far from its old policy of confining defense spending to less that 1% of GNP. Long before the January 24, 1987 Cabinet decision, Japanese defense outlays hovered close to 1%. Military spending for fiscal 1987, for example, will reach $22 billion under the new plan, or 1.004% of GNP.

Symbols are important in Japan and government leaders recognized that they had discarded a respected policy. But they also recognized that with the Japanese economy slowing down in recent years, it had become clear that it was virtually impossible for Japan to meet its stated military goals while at the same time staying under the 1% ceiling.

The policy of abandoning the 1% ceiling is characteristic of the step-by-step approach to change that often seems inconsequential to many foreigners. Yet it falls within a familiar pattern that can eventually lead to significant shifts in policy. Mr. Nakasone, a bold leader by Japanese standards and a long-time advocate of a stronger defense, appears to have viewed the breaching of the 1% barrier as the capstone to a series of changes he has pressed since taking office. However, he is being very careful not to move too fast and too far. The constraints on Japanese defense policy still place a substantial brake on defense spending.

Regardless of the large outlay requirements of Japan's defense goals, substantial increases will be politically unacceptable. As Okazaki Hisahiko, a senior official of the Foreign Ministry and a security specialist put it, since the Finance Ministry and the Diet are accustomed to spending only a small percent of the national budget on defense, in annual budget negotiations it is difficult for any ministry to increase its share of the budget, even 1%. (The JDA has been averaging about a 6% increase over the past few years). As long as the public does not want a drastic change, politicians will not press for one. Also, the nature of Diet debate tends to produce inertia. Government policy is always expressed cautiously. The Opposition or the press never fails to question any new wording. Any expression, particularly one with restrictive implications, once uttered in the Diet is likely to solidify into an official government position and to eventually join the family of built-in restrictions.

Mr. Okazaki concludes that it is always prudent for any strategist or scholar in international affairs to assume that Japan will change very slowly and to build his strategy or premise on that basis. 1.

The 1% issue teaches us that there is, as Okazaki suggests, a deep reluctance to spend the necessary funds to build up Japan's defense capability. This reluctance translates into policies that are having unfortunate consequences for Japanese military effectiveness - slow growth, failure to meet target goals and an inability to respond more positively to U.S. urgings for greater equity in burden-sharing.

Chapter 7

A Case Study - The FY 1985 Defense Budget

It is my purpose to provide a better understanding of the budget process in order that U.S. policymakers can work more effectively with influential Japanese bureaucrats and politicians in building the U.S.-Japan defense relationship. This case study will provide a budget chronology, note the main participants in the process and their level of influence, how they interact in working up the budget, discuss the methodology of budget preparation and describe some of the atmospherics of budget negotiations.

While the amount of the defense budget changes from year to year, (for example, the FY 1984 budget was Y2,934.1 billion and the FY 1985 figure was Y3,137.1 billion), the schedule of budget preparation does not change. The military services, the Internal Bureaus, the Finance Ministry, the LDP, the NDC, and other interested parties must all comply with a formal schedule of events. The JDA and the Finance Ministry are the principals in negotiating the budget, but MITI and the Foreign Ministry enter discussions when procurement and foreign policy considerations are debated. (See Table 9 for a calender of budget preparation).

In compiling the FY 1985 budget, the first major task was to have a committee of senior JDA officials develop a broad substantive outline of budget objectives. The committee began work in early April and after key decisions were made involving improvement in communications and command control, increases in the amount of ammunition available, and strengthening ASDF and MSDF capability,the three military services were directed to prepare draft budgets following the guidelines established by senior officials.

As work progressed, service personnel consulted with officials in the Defense Policy Bureau who were responsible for bringing the military budget in line with the guidelines of senior officials. The service representatives also conferred with officials in the Finance Bureau.

After the military services completed their drafts, they were submitted to the Internal Bureaus for review. Internal Bureau recommendations were then incorporated into the drafts, the three budgets consolidated into one budget, and discussions in the JDA began on establishing a figure for the percentage increase over the previous year's budget. Principal discussants were senior counsellors, the Directors General of the Defense Policy, Finance and Equipment Bureaus and the Administrative Vice Minister. Informal discussions were also held with the Finance Ministry's Budget Bureau, MITI, and LDP politicians at several levels to gain a better sense of an acceptable budget increase.

After senior JDA officials tentatively agreed on a figure, the budget went back to the military services for necessary adjustments. Key budget analysts in the GSDF, ASDF, and MSDF consulted with their counterparts in the Defense Policy Bureau to determine where the adjustments could be made. On reaching agreement, the final defense budget was drafted in the Finance Bureau of JDA, approved by the senior group and the Director General, and formally transmitted

Table 9 — Calendar for Budget Preparaton — JDA

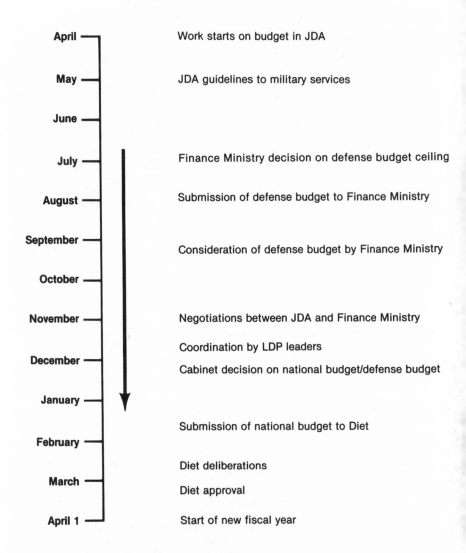

April	Work starts on budget in JDA
May	JDA guidelines to military services
June	
July	Finance Ministry decision on defense budget ceiling
August	Submission of defense budget to Finance Ministry
September	Consideration of defense budget by Finance Ministry
October	
November	Negotiations between JDA and Finance Ministry
December	Coordination by LDP leaders Cabinet decision on national budget/defense budget
January	
February	Submission of national budget to Diet
March	Diet deliberations Diet approval
April 1	Start of new fiscal year

Source: Japan Defense Agency, 1985

54.

to the Finance Ministry in late August.

During work on the budget in JDA from early April to August, Internal Bureau officials sought informal opinions of other agency bureaucrats and LDP politicians and also informed them of the trends in budget thinking within the Agency. The JDA maintained these contacts and sought advice from influential politicians and bureaucrats, in order to lay the groundwork for later negotiations with the Finance Ministry.

As the task of budget preparation went forward within JDA, events were occurring outside that were to have a significant effect on the progress of negotiations. Prior to establishing a national budget ceiling, the Finance Ministry's budget bureau conducted discussions with government agencies to assess their budget needs. JDA Vice Minister Natsume's initial responsibility was to convey to Mr. Matoba, the Deputy Director of the Budget Bureau in the Finance Ministry, the funding requirements for the Agency in FY 1985. Further discussions were then held between Mr. Kato, the Director General of JDA and Mr. Takeshita, the Minister of Finance to gain an understanding on the size of the defense budget. The JDA also briefed the Chief Cabinet Secretary and pro-defense LDP members to gain their support for the hard-bargaining sessions with the Finance Ministry over the percentage increase to be allowed. Mr. Kato and Mr. Takeshita also continued to meet to reach agreement on the formal budget ceiling for the JDA.

As July approached and the Finance Ministry gained a better estimate of government revenues for the year, a recommendation was made to the Cabinet on a ceiling for the national budget which also contained individual ceilings for the various government agencies. The Cabinet approved the overall ceiling on July 31 and each agency had then to re-examine its budget to comply with the Cabinet's decision.

The defense budget was again re-worked in the JDA after lengthy discussions among the three services and the Internal Bureaus. When final agreement was reached, the formal budget was submitted to the Finance Ministry as noted above.

After the submission, the JDA embarked on a promotional campaign to persuade key LDP members, business leaders and top government officials to support the increase desired. Meanwhile, Internal Bureau officials and representatives of the military services were holding discussions with Finance Ministry budget bureau members in efforts to get cuts restored for special projects. These activities took place during the period September - December, 1984.

As time neared for NDC and Cabinet action on the defense budget, JDA lobbying became more intense. Officials stepped up their briefings to gain the backing of government leaders and LDP members for the percentage increase desired.

Inasmuch as Japan's GNP had grown about 4% in the early 1980s, the JDA, in submitting its FY 1985 budget, used this figure in its calculations and decided to request nearly an 8% increase over FY 1984. The Finance Ministry proposed less than a 4% increase. It soon became evident during negotiations that the percentage difference between the two was frozen at about 3.5% and that a final resolution would require a political decision.

A graphic description of how this political decision was made was recounted by a reporter of the *Asahi Shimbun* in a December 29, 1984 article. After the Finance Ministry and the JDA failed to resolve their differences over the amount of increase to be allowed for FY 1985, negotiations began among the

Ministers of Finance and Foreign Affairs, the Director General of JDA, the Director General of the Administrative Management Agency and the four top LDP leaders. The Finance Minister and the Director General of the Administrative Management Agency joined in opposing the JDA request for a 7.20% increase, arguing that at most the increase should not exceed 6.5%. The Minister of Foreign Affairs, invoking the United States-Japan Security Treaty and stressing the need for close defense relations with the United States, said that it was necessary to raise the amount to 6.9%. As no agreement was reached, the LDP Policy Board Chairman recommended that the Prime Minister, who was described as waiting by the telephone in his Official Residence, be asked to decide the issue. Whereupon, a call was placed to the Prime Minister and on signal he indicated that he wished to have the increase at 6.9%. So the issue was closed and the Diet in February 1985 voted the 6.9% increase in the defense budget in "deference to Mr. Nakasone's promise to President Reagan."

This scenario was designed to demonstrate leadership by the Prime Minister in defense policy and to show the United States that Japan would carry out its commitments to build its defense capability. It was also finely orchestrated to gain public acceptence and neutralize opposition to the defense budget.

The dilemma facing Japanese leaders in managing the nation's security policy was again demonstrated. To have accepted the JDA's request for a 7.2% increase, would very likely have breached the 1% barrier and aroused public concern. It would also have brought cries from the media and opposition political parties that the Prime Minister was taking Japan back to militarism. However, to have agreed with the Finance Ministry that the increase should be under 6.5% would have reduced the ability of the JDA to meet defense goals and very probably brought criticism from the United States that Japan was not doing its fair share to defend itself.

Lessons to be learned in this case study are lessons of power and the oftentimes dilemma in exercising that power, of the influence of key players in the budget process and of how tradition and custom provide the rules of the game that politicians and bureaucrats ignore at considerable peril to their careers. As one senior Japanese official who has participated in the defense budget process for many years expressed it, negotiations over the 15% portion of the budget are, in a sense, playacting or an annual ritual with all parties knowing what they must do and about where the negotiations will come out. The hard decisions, he said, have already been made at the division chief level in the three military services, in the Internal Bureaus and the Finance Ministry, and bureaucratic custom dictates that these decisions can be reversed only in the most extreme circumstances and only after careful negotiations. The charade, as he described it, is intended to satisfy political parties, the public and the media that hard bargaining went into the final decision over the defense budget. Appearance, he concluded, thus took on a reality of its own.

While this might appear to be an attempt to place a cloak of inscrutability around the defense budget process, there is considerable truth to the assertion that difficult budget decisions are made at the division chief level in the bureaucracy; that previous budget formats provide valuable guidelines for the next year's negotiations; and that politicians are increasingly projecting themselves into the defense budget process, due in part to the strong influence and leadership given by Prime Minister Nakasone. Political leaders must also bear responsibility for maintaining viable security relations with the United States. As long as Mr. Nakasone remains Prime Minister, opponents of substantial annual increases in the JDA budget will remain on the defensive and be unable to make a significant dent in defense appropriations.

Most Japanese defense analysts believe the LDP election victory in July 1986 assures the continued trend of a 6 to 7% annual increase in the defense budget. While such growth in the past has not exceeded the 1% cap on defense spending, authorities expect that under the new 5-year defense plan and barring a substantial slowdown in the economy, expenditures will move beyond 1% in FY 1987 but by a small margin. [This, in fact, happened as iterated in Chapter 6.]

Maintaining the upward movement in defense spending, the Cabinet on December 28, 1985, approved a $267.8 billion national budget for FY 1986 with defense spending set at $16.5 billion or a 6.58% increase over FY 1985. This kept total defense spending at just under 1% of the Gross National Product.

However, the Ministry of Finance sliced certain equipment requests from the Defense Agency's preliminary FY 1986 budget to pare down its initial request from 7% to 6.6%. The Ministry achieved savings through reduced purchase of helicopters and F-15 aircraft. The defense spending plan for FY 1986 includes major purchases such as 12 F-15 jet fighters, 10 P-3C anti-submarine patrol planes, 4 Patriot surface-to-air guided missile batteries and 3 new destroyers.

The FY 1987 defense budget reflects the realignment sought by Prime Minister Nakasone, who favors a major reorientation toward the air and maritime forces. The Ground Self Defense Force, by far the largest service, is a contradiction to many analysts who note that reliance on home-based ground forces is the equivalent of no defense at all.

Yet the combination of sensitivity over increasing the range of the Self Defense Forces beyond Japan and the political "clout" of the Ground Self Defense Forces within the bureaucracy has meant resistence to significant changes in the relative budget mix of the three services.

Chapter 8

Conclusion

Japanese foreign policy is always subject to intense self-examination. While generally satisfied to play a passive role in foreign affairs, Japan senses that it should be more active internationally. Japan is now reconsidering her passivity because of concern over the relative decline of American military power vis- a- vis the Soviet Union in the Western Pacific; because of her awareness of her own increasing strengths; and because of her intense sensitivity to criticism, especially from the United States, that she is not fulfilling her responsibilities in the trade and defense fields.

This shifting awareness of the world around her has set in motion changes in attitudes about defense and the United States-Japan security relationship. Growing apprehension over the Soviet military buildup on Japan's doorstep and concern about the credibility of the American commitment to defend Japan are in part responsible for this changing mood. This is happening against a background of post-war pacifism and a "peace" constitution that has yielded a relatively ineffective military establishment and produced growing strains in United States-Japan security relations.

Despite public curiosity and concern about the role Japan should play on the international scene, there is little prospect, given the political framework of the defense debate, that Japan will move swiftly to assume new responsibilities in security affairs. The guiding principle of Japanese politics is still the pacifist ideal and the Opposition is alert to any move by the government to depart from Article 9 of the Constitution.

Japanese defense is institutionally wedded to the United States-Japan Security Treaty and is conceptualized to be dependent on American support. The SDF is limited in size and scope because of this dependency relationship and by domestic considerations. It is a policy that has had public support and political and bureaucratic acquiescence. It is also a policy that is increasingly at odds with the reality of security conditions in the Western Pacific and is at the root of the dilemma faced by Japan's leaders in managing defense.

Other constraints, as I noted in Chapter 2, have also worked to limit the role of the SDF. One of the more serious is Japan's delicate financial situation. For several years the country has been living with an austere national budget and, despite urgings from some members of the Liberal Democratic Party, it is not likely that financial restrictions will be eased. Japan's cumulative budget deficit is nearly $600 billion or over 40% of GNP. This compares with about 38% of GNP required to service the U.S. cumulative budget deficit. Despite the deficit, the JDA has enjoyed annual budget increases over the past several years but not enough to remedy the shortage of ammunition, spare parts and petroleum capacity; or the weakness in logistics and communication that encumber the military; or the obsolescence of most artillery, anti-tank weapons and tanks, thereby reducing the capability of the armed forces. The allocation of funds for new equipment for the Maritime and Air Self Defense Forces, in particular, has been inadequate to implement NDPO objectives. According to some estimates, if the procurement goals of NDPO are to be met on schedule,defense spending will have to rise to 1.3% of GNP or more over the next four or five years.

The NDPO is another problem. It was born in detente and its philosophy has been to stress the importance of a "peaceful" SDF. Its ambivalent nature has produced a weapons'procurement policy rather irrelevant to SDF mission responsibilities. The policy has also been exploited by bureaucrats and politicians who wish to keep a brake on defense spending and prevent the security issue from becoming too controversial.

The NDPO makes inadequate provision for training and equipment of military forces and this has hobbled the SDF and caused serious delays in meeting military goals. The MSDF, for example, is confined to coastal surveillance and defense, mainly against enemy submarines. The mission of the ASDF is limited to surveillance and defense of Japan's airspace. ASDF assistance to the GSDF is confined to interdicting amphibious landings and to a limited role in transporting GSDF personnel. JDA basic strategy under the NDPO is to expect an attack against Hokkaido, the northernmost of Japan's four main islands. This is where a majority of the GSDF is stationed and where conditions are being readied for resistance. Studies have shown, however, that attacks on Hokkaido by enemy forces would overwhelm Japanese defenders in a short time. These revelations have been used by the Ground Self Defense Forces to argue for an increased budget to modernize ground forces. Several retired JDA officials told me that without an integrated defense of Hokkaido using air and naval units in close support of ground units, the GSDF, alone, despite modernization, would be unable to defend Hokkaido against a sustained enemy assualt. Even with a well coordinated defense, it would be difficult for the Self Defense Forces to successfully defend Hokkaido without U.S. support and given the present state of their military readiness.

The NDPO also stipulates that the ASDF should have a certain number of planes and the MSDF a specified number of ships. But there is no allowance for trained pilots, ammunition, fuel, protection of airfields and modern communication systems.

The adequate number of torpedoes and other weapons that should be a part of the MSDF arsenal has been underestimated. Such conditions exemplify the peacetime strategy of the NDPO and do not answer the question whether Japanese military forces can actually be used successfully to defend Japan.

The NDPO has given defense planners a relatively free hand to interpret its meaning because of its vagueness as a blueprint for an effective defense buildup. This is a sharp departure from the pre-1976 period when defense planning was more rigid and detailed and there was greater correlation between the SDF mission and the capability of the SDF to carryout that mission. [Ironically, the new 5-year defense plan approved September 18, 1985 as official government policy returns to the pre-1976 defense buildup policy.]

Despite the NDPO shortcomings, it is doubtful that major changes will be forthcoming. The NDPO has been established policy for a decade and it would be inconsistent with postwar government actions to change a major national policy, especially one so controversial, at an early date. Japanese policy has emphasized consistency as a symbol of validity with significant changes in policy direction taken only when there is positive public support, especially when a policy is in serious dispute.

Lacking this support, the government will probably opt for the status quo. Pro-defense groups within the LDP have undertaken several studies to change the NDPO but little has come of these efforts. No major faction leader has advocated change, and without such support, little progress can be made. There is general agreement that the political costs to the LDP of initiating major changes in the NDPO or seeking its outright abolition would be prohibitive. A majority of the public supports keeping the status quo and until the public mood shifts, The NDPO will remain unchanged.

Most influential LDP leaders, including several ex-prime ministers, also seem to be concerned about maintaining a ceiling on defense spending. Prime Minister Nakasone is a notable exception. Yet few of these leaders appear overly worried whether the present level of spending will provide security for the Japanese people. Suggestions that SDF units lack ammunition to withstand an attack lasting more than a few days or that pilots are given inadequate training because of the expense involved are either shrugged off or ignored by the media or treated by politicians as too sensitive to be thoroughly aired in Diet debate.

Adding to the general security problem is uncertainty over U.S. insistence that Japan share more of the defense burden. While discussions have proceeded over Japan's agreement to do more about air and sea surveillance, defense planners remain unsure about the scope of these missions, their cost, their legal sanctions and how the defense budget can sustain these new responsibilities.

Yet Prime Minister Nakasone, almost alone among LDP leaders and top officials of the goverenment, has been receptive to U.S. requests that Japan control the seas south to the Philippines, develop a capability to mine and blockade the straits connecting the Sea of Japan with the Pacific, and build an air defense screen across Japan to interdict Soviet long-range bombers and tactical aircraft. Whether Nakasone can deliver on these requests given the NDPO is uncertain.

There are some encouraging signs. The government apparently felt confident enough to reply to an Opposition member's question in the Diet on February 6, 1986 to the effect that the Constitution would not limit Japan's military support of U.S. efforts to protect Japanese commercial shipping from enemy attacks in sealanes outside Japan's territorial waters. Also, there is increasing talk inside and outside the Diet about using the Self Defense Forces in an "International Emergency Rescue Corps". While none of these developments in themselves can be considered departures from the cautious attitude of Japanese about the Self Defense Forces operating outside Japan, the fact that they are now being openly discussed and debated portends a slow shift in public attitude toward greater acceptence of a more active security role for Japan in cooperation with the United States.

This new plateau of discussion has not materially affected the problems besetting defense planners. Adding to their difficulties has been the impact of the MTPE on defense policy. Constant slippage in meeting defense goals has been a by-product of MTPE; there is very little the planners can do to stop the hemorrhage. The new 5 year plan, which incorporates the 59 MTPE procurement outline, calls for the purchase of 187 F-15 Eagle fighters and 100 P3C antisubmarine aircraft, among other things, that will have to be paid for by a defense budget that Mr. Nakasone has had to promise will not exceed 1% of GNP in FY 1986. This will inevitably result in further deferred payments.

Mr. Nakasone's advocacy of the new 5 year plan is a way, as he sees it, of avoiding the annual controversy over the 1% cap on defense spending. He succeeded in persuading party leaders to approve the new plan but initially failed to obtain their agreement to remove the 1% ceiling. Senior party officials, tactically allied against Nakasone, argued that there was no immediate need to change the 1% policy and that to do so would cause political repercussions. An

August 1985 poll showed that an overwhelming majority of Japanese favored retaining the 1% ceiling. However, despite these obstacles, Nakasone, as I noted, succeeded in removing the 1% cap on defense spending in January 1987, but not by much - 1.04% of GNP.

The results of the poll would appear to be overtaken by the national election of July 6,1986, wherein the Socialist Party, the principal opponent of change in the 1% policy, suffered a crushing defeat and the LDP emerged with a substantial majority in both Houses of the Diet. The effectiveness of Opposition tactics to stymie Mr. Nakasone's plans to buildup the SDF and seek closer military ties with the United States will probably be reduced.

The new 5 year plan, like its predecessors, is flawed in that it lacks a conceptual framework within which Japanese defense strategy can be formulated in precise terms so that the public can better understand defense policy objectives and the need for adequate funds to meet such objectives.

Another weakness in the defense structure is the JDA's lack of bureaucratic stature and prestige. In the tough world of Japanese bureaucracy, the JDA cannot compete for influence with the powerful Finance Ministry, the Ministry of International Trade and Industry and the outside interests they represent. These outside organizations range from Keidanren, Japan's powerful economic organization representing major industries and companies, to the big banks and other financial institutions that believe their best interests lie elsewhere than in defense.

Constitutional and legal restrictions also handicap advocates of a more forceful defense program. Article 9, as I have noted, curtails enthusiasm for a more vigorous defense effort. Article 9 and the public consensus that supports it place heavy burdens on the SDF in planning strategy and tactics for the defense of Japan. The selection of weapon systems, for example, is of particular concern. What is an offensive weapon? What is a defensive one? Countless hours are spent in Diet debate explaining this vexing problem.

General interpretation of the Constitution over the past several decades has placed severe prohibitions on the development and use of so-called offensive weapons. While no specific laws exist to limit their use, their prohibition has been institutionalized in custom and tradition. Using them in offensive operations would require a reorientation in public thinking on defense of Japan; an unlikely prospect. Reinterpretation of Article 9 to allow more flexibility in Japan's defense planning will take time.

Japan's concern about how her neighbors will react to an ambitious defense program makes her cautious. While, as I have noted, opinions differ in ASEAN countries and in China and Korea about Japanese rearmament, a common worry is that Japan will become too strong. In discussing defense policy with American officials, Japanese often stress this worry to justify their own modest defense effort.

While the Japanese are becoming anxious about Russian saber-rattling, they appear convinced that the Soviet Union has no intention of invading Japan. Intention is an important crucible for judging behavior in Japan. It is the perception of the "threat" that the Soviet Union poses, however, that beclouds United States-Japan security relations.

The Russian military buildup in East Asia is real and both nations must be prepared to respond. The United States will be obliged to earmark certain units for the defense of Japan and both nations will have to agree on what constitutes an emergency. The United States and Japan, in the words of Professor Nathaniel Thayer, are going to have to give more and get less and are going to have to turn the Security Treaty into an agreement which deals with the real Soviet threat and a credible response. 1.

Viewed from another perspective, there needs to be enough realization of the threat to induce the Japanese to increase their forces for the defense of their homeland. So long as the United States maintains its military strength in the area to meet the Soviet challenge, Japanese concern about their safety is much less than it would be if the United States told them frankly that there is a limit to what America can do to defend Japan, given its global commitments. Japan could then draw its own conclusions by what she perceives in terms of United States and Soviet forces.

But even as Japanese listen to the speeches of frustrated Congressmen and Senators, who call for the reduction of U.S. forces available to defend Japan as a way of pressuring the Japanese to spend more on their own security, there is little evidence that these remonstrances are changing many minds in Japan about the "threat" from the Soviet Union. Of equal importance, nothing would worry U.S. policymakers more, especially those in the Pentagon, than the prospect of losing critical military bases in Japan. The Japanese are well aware of this and are thus generally unmoved by Congressional admonishments.

These two approaches to the "threat" have built-in hazards for the relationship. Spurring Japan to build a stronger SDF against public opposition runs the risk of creating political instability and a backlash of animosity and resentment against the United States. Threatening Japan with the possibility of limiting the American commitment under the Security Treaty could unleash a storm of anti-American sentiment that would pose dangers to our bases in Japan. The Soviets could complicate the issue further by indicating a willingness to reach an accommodation with Japan on key problems such as the Northern Islands. Such a change in Soviet tactics would make it more difficult for Mr. Nakasone or his successor to continue to build momentum under the rearmament program. This would surely result in an exacerbation of feeling in the United States and Japan over the security relationship. The dilemma for Japanese defense planners is real and vexing.

The most important constraint on the defense buildup is public opinion which for the past decade has slowly changed from non-acceptance of the SDF to full acceptance but with the important caveat that the buildup proceed slowly. This cautious attitude is a mixture of concern about resurgent militarism, a strong belief in the appropriateness of Article 9 of the Constitution, and a reluctance to spend more than the minimum necessary to insure continued American support. These public expressions of prudence in defense management are dutifully noted by politicians who are hesitant to comply with the urgings of the United States for an accelerated defense buildup that exceeds what they believe the public will tolerate. Yet, paradoxically, the public, which poll after poll reveals to be lukewarm on defense, has given Prime Minister Nakasone a remarkable popularity rating, [and a notable July 1986 election victory], considering that he is probably the most nationalistic and militarily realistic leader to have come on the political scene in the last quarter century.

Japanese defense policy, as Professor Curtis notes, needs to be seen within the context of basic Japanese orientations to international affairs, orientations that are rooted in the country's profound sense of vulnerability given its dependence on the outside world for raw materials and markets. Despite dramatic changes in Japan's economic position and a growing sense that Japan should play a more active role in international affairs, basic Japanese orientations to international politics continue to emphasize minimizing risks, revealing the propensity to define foreign policy issues in terms of how Japan can best react and adjust to situations created by others rather than in terms of how Japan itself can contribute to the structuring of the international system. 2.

These attitudes are deeply ingrained in Japanese politics and the political, bureaucratic and business leadership. One consequence, insofar as defense policy is concerned, is a tendency to debate defense issues in terms of what needs to be done to deal with American demands rather than to formulate an independent national security policy.

The United States-Japan Security Treaty gives Japan the protection to grow economically and thereby secure a better life for her people. The treaty also provides benefits for the United States that are sometimes overlooked in the heat of arguments over Japan's defense buildup. The United States has received a forward base from which it may be possible to operate in the event of renewed hostilities in Korea, an advanced logistical and industrial system that may be called upon in times of emergency, and a base for stability in Northeast Asia that has been enhanced over the past several decades through close U.S.-Japan cooperation. The U.S. presence in Japan has not only given the Japanese the sense of security that they desperately want in the face of growing Soviet military power, but it has also introduced caution into Soviet military and political actions in the area.

Security cooperation between the two countries can be further advanced through greater knowledge on the United States' part of how the Japanese defense establishment functions, the principal power bases in the establishment, and the role of the bureaucrat and politician in defense policy. This investigation of Japan's defense policy has attempted to shed some light on these considerations.

The study began by making certain assumptions about U.S.-Japan defense policy followed by recommendations for developing closer and more effective security ties. The main thrust of the assumptions was that Japan will move slowly and cautiously in building up her defense forces and that U.S. influence to hasten the process is limited.

Instances were elucidated in which U.S. requests for a greater Japanese effort to achieve equity in defense burden sharing were met by procrastination and genuine concern about how to deal with U.S. demands.

At the root of the policy dilemma for Japan's leaders is the political reality of a highly skeptical electorate, nervous over any signs of a government move to accelerate the pace of the arms buildup, and of a suspicious, dovish media that is quick to censure the government's defense plans.

Some labor unions (especially Sohyo), religious groups, academicians, and the so-called "floating voter" with no party affiliation but resistent to rearmament, coalesce around opposition parties (Socialist, Democratic Socialist, Komeito, and the Communists) and are another source of concern to leaders of the ruling LDP. The party is sensitive to any accusation that it might impose its will through the discredited tactic of practicing "the tyranny of the majority", the political maneuver that led to the downfall of the Kishi Government in 1960. These considerations reinforce the dilemma felt by government leaders in seeking a rational defense policy.

Judging from past history and barring unforeseen emergencies, Japan's defense buildup will continue to be slow and measured. Yet if one looks closely, there appears to be a gradual awakening by government leaders that Japan must assume more responsibility for her own defense, befitting a nation that has grown in power and prestige over the past several decades. According to one high official, such a re-examination of Japan's security role in her relations with the United States would have to take into account the U.S.-Japan Security Treaty, perhaps modifying the Treaty to equalize commitments. This would take time and would require educating the public on the need for Treaty revision. The task would be formidable, he thought, because Japan, since the end of the Occupation, has grown comfortable with the lop-sided nature of the Security Treaty.

The United States, for its part, must put emphasis on situations where there is a clear relationship between U.S. need for assistance and Japanese actual and potential capabilities to provide such assistance. Broadening the dialogue at various levels will hasten the day when Japan and the United States achieve some parity in burden sharing.

History warns of the consequences of estrangement. In pre-war U.S.-Japan relations, the inability of each side to communicate clearly the core of their national interests and the limits of their tolerance, foreordained ultimate military conflict. In the world of the 1980s and beyond, we should look back and see where we and the Japanese failed to resolve differences. We should identify our common interests more clearly by close and effective collaboration on the vital issues of peace and security in the Western Pacific.

It is in our mutual interest to preserve a satisfactory security relationship; to minimize friction and tension that lap at the shores of our common concern for peace. For if we have learned anything from history and from the present international environment, it is that America and Japan need each other.

The national security of the United States must be grounded in a clear, unobstructed view of what is necessary to preserve our way of life. Translated into the practical politics of U.S.-Japan relations, it means that we must have the continued support of Japan for our military presence there and the use of joint forces in defense of our mutual interests and that we must reinforce the credibility of our security commitment to the Japanese. Pending the reformation of human nature, the U.S. national interest must continue to be the centerpiece of our foreign policy and of our relations with Japan.

Japanese leaders pressured from within to be conciliatory and cautious and from without to be energetic and positive in delivering on policy promises, need the assurances that only close and fruitful collaboration with the United States at various policy levels can provide. If we ignore the lessons of history, we will be ill-equipped to keep the peace in the Western Pacific.

History has also shown that effective cooperation between states depends to a considerable extent on the personal relations between leaders. President Reagan and Prime Minister Nakasone have established close, personal ties that have helped to enrich the relationship. But important leadership changes are in prospect for both countries. President Reagan and Prime Minister Nakasone will shortly give way to their successors. As Nakasone nears the end of his tenure as Prime Minister, slated to be in October 1987, speculation has already begun about who in the LDP will succeed him and what changes, if any, will occur in Japanese defense policy. Nakasone has been the leader among postwar Prime Ministers in urging a buildup of Japan's Self Defense Forces. He has overcome resistence from the leaders in his own party . He shrewdly judged the climate right to make a change, albeit small, in defense policy by eliminating the 1% ceiling on defense spending. Adverse public reaction to the change was less than many analysts had expected. Nakasone has thus set the course for his successor to follow. The question on many minds in Japan is will the next Prime Minister be as vigorous in supporting the Self Defense Forces.

The three LDP politicians considered most likely to succeed Nakasone are Abe Shintaro, the former Foreign Minister, Takeshita Noboru, the former Finance Minister, and Miyazawa Kiichi, the present Finance Minister. Abe has assumed the leadership of the former Fukuda faction, Takeshita has recently broken away from the Tanaka faction and formed his own group, and Miyazawa has inherited direction of the former Suzuki faction. The latest polls show that Abe is leading his fellow contenders, but not by much.

The next Prime Minister is not expected to be as forceful an advocate as Nakasone of a strong defense force. He will probably maintain a relatively "low posture" on defense, barring unforeseen developments in the power balance in East Asia, but, like Nakasone, will continue to opt for close security relations with the United States.

Epilogue

The Strategic Defense Initiative (SDI)

Evidence continues to grow of close and fruitful military cooperation between the Self Defense Forces and American military units in Japan. The recent agreement of Japan to share military technology with the United States shows a further determination of the two countries to work together in the security field. This has not been accomplished without some uncertainty by Japanese officials that a too close relationship might involve Japan in U.S. disputes with the Soviet Union and other Communist countries. Nevertheless, cooperation is felt to be in the best interests of the two sides and prompted the United States to invite Japan to join with Great Britain and West Germany in research on America's strategic defense initiative program.

On September 9, 1986, the Japanese Cabinet agreed in principle for Japan to join the SDI program subject to negotiations with the United States on conditions for participation. There was general agreement among Japanese leaders to permit private companies and research institutes to take part in the missile-defense program.

Although U.S. officials have insisted that Japanese involvement is not critical for the space defense project to succeed, they hoped to benefit from Japan's advances in electronics, lasers, and rocket propulsion. Japanese industry, in turn, has steadily grown more eager to join the research, largely out of concern about falling behind in developing technologies. That worry increased after Great Britain and West Germany announced they would take part in the program. The likelihood that Japan would also say yes to the project rose sharply when a Government and industry study group said participation would promise valuable "spinoffs." Some estimates are that Japanese contractors could obtain as much as 15% of the $26 billion projected as the project's budget for the first five years. Japan's participation would also help to promote closer security relations and cooperation in technology transfer.

Both governments announced that Japan would join SDI under a formal agreement signed on July 21, 1987. It would provide for private Japanese companies to participate in SDI research. Japan becomes the fifth country to conclude a government-to-government arrangement with the United States on SDI research, following Great Britain, West Germany, Italy and Israel. The U.S.-Japan agreement provides for Japanese firms to use research data, subject to individual agreement with the U.S. Department of Defense, and to maintain the confidentiality of research data in accordance with the U.S.-Japan Mutual Defense Assistance Agreement.

The FY1987 Defense Budget

JDA has proposed a defense budget of Y3,554.1 billion or about $23 billion at the exchange rate of 150/1 for FY 1987 which is designed to achieve most of the targets in the second year of the new 5-year plan. The budget gives high priority to improving air and sea defense capabilities, including those for protecting the 1,000 mile sealane extending from the Japanese coast to Guam and the Northern Philippines. Most of the military frontline equipment will be purchased on a deferred payment basis with payments to start after FY 1988. The JDA deferred payment debt will reach Y2,793.6 billion, or $18 billion, in FY1987.

The 1986 Defense White Paper

The Government issued the 1986 Defense White Paper on August 8, 1986 and it immediately drew criticism from the media. The major complaint dealt with the failure of the report to explain what the government intends to do about achieving the goals set in the National Defense Program Outline (NDPO). While the report was rather specific on the nature of the growing threat from the Soviet military buildup in the Western Pacific, it was vague and sketchy on what steps Japan should take to counter the threat. Also criticized was the lack of information about the Goverenment's intention to revise the NDPO, only hints, said the *Japan Times Weekly* of August 30, 1986, that the Government might sooner or later have to make adjustments in the NDPO to cope with changing international conditions. To treat such an important subject in this manner, said the *Japan Times Weekly*, is to do a disservice to the public whose support is necessary before any changes in the NDPO can be undertaken.

Pressure from Senator Robert Byrd, the Senate Majority Leader

The *Hokubei Mainichi* of August 28, 1986 reported that Senator Byrd sent a letter to President Reagan on August 26, 1986 demanding that Japan take specific action to increase its defense capability. Specifically, he proposed that the Japanese purchase U.S. military equipment to accelerate the improvement of the SDF and meet the objectives of the new 5-year defense plan. He also said that President Reagan should urge Japan to shoulder about $300 million in wages now paid annually by the U.S. government for Japanese civilians working at U.S. bases in Japan. Senator Byrd further advocated that Japan should fully fund the 2nd year of the 5-year defense plan to insure at least a 5.4% real growth in its defense expenditures in FY1987 and re-examine the NDPO. This is another example of the kind of pressure exerted on Japanese policymakers that has led to the dilemma in managing Japan's defense.

July 1987

Appendix A.

Persons Interviewed

1. AKA, Raymond, American Embassy
2. FUJII, Kazuo, Japan Defense Agency
3. FUYUTSUME, Toshinori, Japan Defense Agency
4. IMAIZUMI, Takehisa, Japan Defense Agency
5. INOKI, Masamichi, President, Research Institute for Peace and Security
6. ISAYAMA, Takeshi, Ministry of International Trade and Industry
7. ITO, Keiichi, Advisor, Mitsubishi Electric Corporation
8. ITO, Kenichi, Aoyama Gakuin University
9. IWASHIMA, Hisao, National Institute for Defense Studies
10. JOHNSON, Colonel Robert, American Embassy, Tokyo
11. KAIHARA, Osamu, former high official of the Japan Defense Agency
12. KANEKO, Kumao, Japan Institute for International Affairs
13. KASAGI, Masaaki, Nihon Shimbun Kyokai
14. KATO, Ryozo, Japanese Foreign Ministry
15. KAWASAKI, Nozomu, Japan Defense Agency
16. MASUZOE, Yoichi, Tokyo University
17. MATSUO, Fumio, Kyodo News Service
18. MIHARA, Asao, Member, Lower House of the Diet
19. NATSUME, Haruo, Vice Minister, Japan Defense Agency
20. NISHIHARA, Masashi, National Defense Academy
21. NOMURA, Iizuru, Finance Ministry
22. ONISHI, Seiichiro, Research Institute for Peace and Security
23. RUBENSTEIN, Gregg, American Embassy, Tokyo
24. SAKAMOTO, Hiroshi, Japan National Press Club
25. SAKANAKA, Tomohisa, Asahi Shimbun/Aoyama Gakuin University
26. SAKATA, Michita, Speaker of the Lower House of the Diet
27. SHIINA, Motoo, Member, Lower House of the Diet
28. SHIOTA, Akira, Secretary General, National Defense Council
29. TANAKA, Akihiko, University of Tokyo
30. TSUBOI, Tatsufumi, National Defense Council
31. USHIBA, Akihiko, Sankei Shimbun
32. WATANABE, Koji, Japanese Foreign Ministry
33. WEINSTEIN, Martin, International University of Japan
34. YAMASHITA, Shintaro, Japanese Foreign Ministry

Appendix B.

Defense Agency Establishment Law
(Partial)

Chapter 1

General Provisions

Article 1 - Purpose of the law

The purpose of the law is to define the scope of responsibility and powers of the Defense Agency and to prescribe an organization suitable for the efficient fulfillment of its mission and also to provide for the establishment of a National Defense Council.

Chapter 2 - Defense Agency
Section 1. General Rules

Article 2 - Establishment
A Defense Agency shall be established as an external bureau of the Prime Minister's Office under the provision of paragraph 2, Article 3 of the National Administrative Organization Law (Law No.120 of 1948). Article 3. Director General. The Chief of the Defense Agency shall be the Director General of the Defense Agency who is a State Minister.

2. The Director General of the Defense Agency (hereinafter referred to as the "Director General") shall, subject to the direction and supervision of the Prime Minister, direct the affairs of the Agency, appoint and dismiss personnel under his jurisdiction (exclusive of personnel of the Procurement Agency) and supervise their performance on duty.

3. A part of the appointment authority as prescribed in the preceding paragraph may be delegated to the senior personnel within the Agency.

Article 4. - Mission of the Defense Agency
The mission of the Defense Agency will be to preserve the peace and independence and to maintain the security of our nation. For this purpose, it shall control and operate the Ground Self Defense Forces, the Maritime Self Defense Forces, and Air Self Defense Forces (refers to the Ground Self Defense Forces, Maritime Self Defense Forces, and Air Self Defense Forces as prescribed in paragraph 2 through 4, Article 2 of the Self Defense Law, Law No. 165 of 1954; hereinafter the same) and to perform functions related thereto.

2. In addition to the mission prescribed in the preceding paragraph, the Defense Agency has the mission of performing the functions as prescribed in Article 3 of the Procurement Agency Establishment Law (Law No. 129 of 1949). Article 5. Power of the Defense Agency. For the purpose of performing the specific functions prescribed in this Law, the Defense Agency shall have the powers enumerated below. Such powers shall, however, be exercised in accordance with laws, including orders issued thereunder:

(1) To perform within the limits of budgetary appropriations, those acts pertaining to expenditures necessary for carrying out its specific functions;

(2) To collect revenues and make payments necessary in carrying out its specific functions;

(3) To establish and maintain offices, camps, maneuver areas, and other facilities directly required for carrying out its specific functions;

(4) To procure equipment, ships, aircraft, subsistence and other supplies (hereinafter generally referred to as "equipment, etc.") and services directly required for carrying out its specific functions;

(5) To dispose of unnecessary property;

(6) To conduct appointment, dismissal, award, and discipline of personnel and administer other than personnel affairs;

(7) To establish and maintain facilities required for the welfare and health of personnel;

(8) To establish and maintain housing to be rented to personnel;

(9) To prepare, distribute, or publish documents, statistics, and research data concerning its specific functions;

(10) To supervise its specific functions and to take such measures as may be required in accordance with the provisions of laws and orders;

(11) To effect dissemination and publicity of its specific functions;

(12) To adopt the official seal of the Defense Agency;

(13) To take action to defend the nation against direct and indirect aggression, to preserve the peace and independence of the nation, and to maintain national security;

(14) To take action in case of special necessity to maintain public peace and order;

(15) To take action in case of special necessity to protect lives and properties or to maintain public peace at sea;

(16) To take action in case of necessity to protect lives and properties in the event of natural disaster, calamity, and other catastrophes;

(17) To remove and dispose of mines and other dangerous explosive objects;

(18) To take measures against violation of the territorial air space;

(19) To receive and undertake civil engineering works, etc., for State and local public organizations, in case the works comply with the purpose of training the Self Defense Forces(refers to the Self Defense Force prescribed in paragraph 1, Article 2 of the Self Defense Forces Law; hereinafter the same);

(20) To conduct necessary investigation and research for the fulfillment of its specific functions;

(21) To conduct necessary education and training for the fulfillment of its specific functions;

(22) Powers prescribed in Article 4 of the Procurement Agency Establishment Law;

(23) In addition to those enumerated in the preceding items, such other powers as placed under the Defense Agency in accordance with laws (including orders issued thereunder).

Article 6 - Self Defense Forces

The mission of the Self Defense Forces, structure and organization of units and organs of the Self Defense Forces, direction and supervision concerning the Self Defense Forces, action and powers, etc., of the Self Defense Forces shall be provided for in the Self Defense Forces Law.

Article 7 - Fixed Number of Personnel

The fixed number (except those who are employed for a fixed term of not more than 2 months, those who are temporarily retired and the part-time employees) of personnel (except the Director General, the Parliamentary Vice

Minister and personnel of the Procurement Agency, hereinafter the same) shall be 268,333.

2. Of the fixed number of personnel in the preceding paragraph, the fixed number of the Self Defense Officials shall be 171,500 for the Self Defense Officials of the Ground Self Defense Force (hereinafter referred to as "Ground Self-Defense Officials"); 32,097 for the Self Defense Officials of the Maritime Self Defense Force (hereinafter referred to as "Maritime Self Defense Officials"); 38,337 for the Self Defense Officials of the Air Self Defense Force (hereinafter referred to as "Air Self Defense Officials"); and the grand total of 242,009 with the aggregation of the number of Ground Self Defense Force Officials, Maritime Self Defense Force Officials, and Air Self Defense Force Officials in the Joint Staff Council.

Article 8 - Deleted

Article 9 - Councillors

There shall be established not more than 9 councillors in the Defense Agency.

2. The councillors, subject to the direction of the Director General, shall assist the Director General in the formulation of basic policy concerning the specific functions of the Defense Agency.

Section 2. Main Agency
Sub-section 1. Internal Sub-Divisions

Article 10.

There shall be the following 6 bureaus in the Main Agency in addition to the Director General's Secretariat:

Defense Bureau
Education Bureau
Personnel Bureau
Medical Bureau
Finance Bureau
Equipment Bureau

Article 11. Specific Functions of the Director General's Secretariat.

The Director General's Secretariat shall take charge of the following functions related to the specific functions of the Defense Agency:

(1) Classified matters;

(2) Custody of the official seals of the Director General and the Defense Agency;

(3) Receipt, dispatch, compilation, and custody of official documents;

(4) Liaison and coordination with each sub division office;

(5) Section organization, fixed number of personnel, and personnel affairs of the internal sub divisions;

(6) Examination of draft legislation and other documents;

(7) Inspection of the administration;

(8) Public information, and

(9) In addition to the matters listed in the preceding items, those functions that are not in the jurisdiction of other sub divisions and offices.

Article 12. Specific Functions of the Defense Bureau.

The Defense Bureau shall administer the following functions:

(1) Basic policy and coordination of defense and operations;

(2) Basic policy related to actions of the Self Defense Forces;

(3) Basic policy related to structure, fixed number of personnel,

organization, equipment and deployment of the Ground Self Defense Forces, the Maritime Self Defense Forces, and the Air Self Defense Forces: and

(4) Collection and adjustment regulation of data and information required for the function in each of the above items.

Article 13. Specific Functions of the Education Bureau.

The Education Bureau shall administer the following functions:

(1) Basic policy related to education and training of personnel; and,

(2) Defense Staff College and Defense Academy.

Article 14. Specific Functions of the Personnel Bureau.

The Personnel Bureau shall administer the following functions:

(1) Appointment and dismissal, status, disciplinary punishment and duty performance of personnel, and other personnel affairs;

(2) Basic policy related to recruiting and welfare of personnel;

(3) System related to ceremonies, award, uniform regulation, compensation of personnel, and

(4) Fair Board

Article 15. Specific Functions of the Finance Bureau.

The Finance Bureau shall administer the following functions:

(1) Estimate of expenditures and revenue, settlement of accounts, accounting, auditing (limited to those related to the Self Defense Forces, hereinafter the same in the subsequent two items);

(2) Basic policy related to accounting for property;

(3) Basic policy related to management of administrative property, acquisition, maintenance and management of facilities, and

(4) Construction office

Article 16. Specific Functions of the Equipment Bureau.

The Equipment Bureau shall administer the following functions:

(1) Basic policy related to procurement, supply, maintenance and custody of equipment, etc. (exclusive of medical material; hereinafter the same in the subsequent items), and procurement services (limited to those related to the Self Defense Forces; hereinafter the same as in subsequent items),

(2) Basic policy related to standardization of specification, research and improvement of equipment, and

(3) Technical Research Office and Procurement Office

Article 17. Personnel of Internal Sub Divisions.

The Director General's Secretariat shall have a Secretary General, and each bureau shall have a Chief of Bureau

2. The Secretary General and the Chiefs of Bureaus shall be councillors.

3. The Secretary General shall, subject to direction, administer the functions of the Director General's Secretariat.

4. The Chiefs of Bureaus shall, subject to direction, administer the functions of the bureaus.

Article 18.

There shall be in the Director General's Secretariat and each bureau, Secretaries, staff members, and other necessary personnel.

2. The Secretaries shall, subject to direction, administer the functions.

3. The staff members shall, subject to direction, participate in the functions.

4. The Secretaries shall be appointed the Section Chiefs of the Director General's Secretariat or if each bureau, or placed in office prescribed in paragraph 3, Article 20 of the National Administrative Organization Law.

Article 19. Duties of Self Defense officials in the Internal Sub Divisions.

The Director General may, when he deems it necessary, have Self Defense Officials of the Ground Staff Office, the Maritime Staff Office, or the Air Staff Office, or Self Defense Officials assigned to units or organs (hereinafter referred to as "units, etc." in this Article and in item 4, paragraph 1 of Article 23), as prescribed in Article 29, serve in the internal sub divisions.

2. The Self Defense Officials as mentioned in the preceding paragraph shall be subject to the direction and supervision of the Chief of the sub division wherein they are ordered to serve in regard to their duties, and to the supervision of the Chief of the Staff Office or unit, etc., to which they are assigned in regard to their status.

Article 20.

Relations between the Secretary General and the Chiefs of Bureaus, and between the Chiefs of Staff and the Joint Staff Council. The Secretary General and the Chiefs of Bureaus shall assist the Director General in the following matters concerning their specific functions:

(1) Instruction of the Director General to the Chief of the Ground Staff, the Chief of the Maritime Staff, or the Chief of the Air Staff with respect to the preparation of various policies and basic implementation plans pertaining to the Ground Self Defense Forces, the Maritime Self Defense Forces, or the Air Self Defense Forces;

(2) Approval of the Director General on the policies and basic implementation plans prepared by the Chief of the Ground Staff, the Chief of the Maritime Staff, or the Chief of the Air Staff with regard to the matters of the Ground Self Defense Forces, the Maritime Self Defense Forces, or the Air Self Defense Forces;

(3) Instruction and approval of the Director General on matters under the jurisdiction of the Joint Staff Council;

(4) General supervision by the Director General over the Ground Self Defense Forces, the Maritime Self Defense Forces, or the Air Self Defense Forces.

Sub Section 2. Staff Office

Article 21. Staff Office.

There shall be established in the main agency a Ground Staff Office, a Maritime Staff Office, and an Air Staff Office (hereinafter simply referred to as "Staff Offices").

2. The Ground Staff Office shall be the Staff organ of the Director General with respect to affairs of the Ground Self Defense Forces; the Maritime Staff Office shall be the Staff organ of the Director General with respect to affairs of the Maritime Self Defense Forces; and the Air Staff Office shall be the Staff organ of the Director General with respect to affairs of the Air Self Defense Forces.

3. There shall be divisions and sections in the Staff Offices.

4. In addition to those prescribed in the preceding paragraphs, the internal organization of the Staff Offices shall be prescribed by a Cabinet Order.

Article 22. Chief of Staff.

The Chief of the Ground Staff Office shall be the Chief of the Ground Staff; the Chief of the Maritime Staff Office shall be the Chief of the Maritime Staff; and the Chief of the Air Staff Office shall be the Chief of the Air Staff.

2. The Chief of the Ground Staff shall be a Ground Self Defense Official; the Chief of the Maritime Staff shall be a Maritime Self Defense Official; and the Chief of the Air Staff shall be an Air Self Defense Official.

3. The Chief of the Ground Staff, the Chief of the Maritime Staff, or the Chief of the Air Staff (hereinafter simply referred to as "Chiefs of Staff") shall, subject to the direction and supervision of the Director General, administer the functions of the Staff Offices.

Article 23. Specific Functions of the Staff Office.

The Ground Staff Office, the Maritime Staff Office, and the Air Staff Office, shall administer the following functions respectively, with regard to the Ground Self Defense Forces, the Maritime Self Defense Forces, and the Air Self Defense Forces:

(1) Preparation of plans for defense and operations;

(2) Preparation of plans for education, training, action, organization, equipment, deployment, information, finance, procurement, supply, health and sanitation, personnel affairs and recruiting of personnel.

Appendix C.
Organization of the National Defense Council

National Defense Council

President: Prime Minister
Members: Deputy Prime Minister
           Minister for Foreign Affairs
           Minister for Finance
           Director General of the Defense Agency
           Director General of the Economic Planning Agency
Regularly Present:
           Minister for International Trade and Industry
           Director General of the Science and Technology Agency
           Chief Cabinet Secretary
           Director General of the Cabinet Legislation Bureau
           Secretary General of ther National Defense Council
Assistant Members:
           Parliamentary Deputy Chief Cabinet Secretary
           Administrative Deputy Chief Cabinet Secretary
           Administrative Vice Minister for Foreign Affairs
           Administrative Vice Minister for Finance
           Administrative Vice Minister, Defense Agency
           Administrative Vice Minister for Economic Planning
           Administrative Vice Minister for International Trade and
           Industry
           Administrative Vice Minister for Science and Technology

Secretariat

               Secretary General
Fulltime   Counselor - defense
               Counselor - political
               Counselor - economy

Counselor (Chief, Security Division, North American Affairs Bureau, Ministry of Foreign Affairs)

Counselor (Budget Examiner, Defense, Budget Bureau, Ministry of Finance)

Concurrent   Counselor (Chief, Defense Planning Division, Defense Policy Bureau, Defense Agency)

Counselor (Senior Planning Officer, Planning Bureau, Economic Planning Agency)

Counselor (Chief, Aircraft and Ordnance Division, Machinery and Information Industries Bureau, Ministry of International Trade and Industry)

Counselor (Chief, General Affairs Division, Minister's Secretariat, Science and Technology Agency)

Assistant Counselors   7
Administrative Officials   10

Appendix D.
The New Mid-Term Planning Estimate (*chugyo*)- 1985
(translation)

I. Medium-Term Defense Power Consolidation Plan

1. **Consolidation Policy.** In consolidating defense power from FY 1986 to FY 1990, the target will be to attain a level of defense power prescribed in the "Defense Plan General Outline" (National Defense Council and Cabinet decision of October 29, 1976). The international military situation and the trends of various nations' technological levels will be considered, and in order to consolidate effective defense power, capable of coping with them, the various kinds of defense functions will be checked in detail, in regard to the GSDF, the MSDF, and the ASDF, respectively, and efforts will be made to allocate resources on a priority basis. Still further, special consideration will be given to the promotion of an organic cooperative setup among the various SDFs.

In promoting concrete projects, importance shall be attached to the following points:

Through strengthening and modernization of equipment, such as aircraft, naval ships, surface-to-air guided missiles, etc., efforts will be made to improve air defense capability for the homeland and the capability to secure the safety of sealanes in the waters surrounding our country. At the same time, taking into consideration the special geographic characteristics of our country, efforts will also be made to improve capabilities to cope with a landing and invasion from the sea and air, through the modernization of the divisions and the diversification of their organization and through strengthening the capability for destruction (of an enemy) on the sea and at the water's edge.

Efforts will be made to consolidate defense power by maintaining balance between frontline and the rear. For this purpose, importance will be attached especially to the improvement of intelligence, reconnaissance, command and communication capabilities, continuous combat capability, immediate response capability and sustainability, and to the promotion of technological research and development. At the same time, consideration will be given to improving proficiency through the education and training systems, etc., and the improvement in the livelihood environment of personnel.

II. Main Contents of Consolidation

1. **Homeland Air Defense Capability.**

(1) In order to strengthen and modernize air defense interception capability, interceptor fighters (F15s) and early warning planes (E2Cs) will be consolidated. At the same time, in regard to improving the capability of interceptor fighters (F4EJs), necessary measures will be taken, after conducting studies separately, to strengthen their combat readiness.

(2) In order to strengthen and modernize air defense fire power in important areas, surface-to-air (Nike-J) guided missiles will be replaced with surface-to-air (Patriot) guided missiles. In addition to the above, equipment for improving surface-to-air (Hawk) guided missiles will be consolidated. Also, short range surface-to-air guided missiles, new anti aircraft machine cannon, etc., will be consolidated.

2. **Capability for the Defense of Surrounding Sea Areas and Capability for Securing the Safety of Sea Lanes.**

(1) For strenthening and modernizing defense capability by naval ships, escort ships, submarines, mine sweepers, missile ships, supply ships, will be

built.

In building escort ships, emphasis will be on equipping them with missiles for strengthening their anti-submarine capability and for improvement of anti-ship and anti-air capabilities.

(2) For strengthening and modernizing defense capability of aircraft, fixed-wing anti-submarine patrol planes (p-3cs), anti-submarine helicopters (to include new shipborne-type anti-submarine helicopters) and mine sweeper helicopters (MH-53Es) will be consolidated.

3. Capability to Cope with Landing and Invasion from Sea and Air.

(1) In order to strengthen on-the-sea and water's edge destruction capabilities, surface-to-ship guided missiles will be consolidated. At the same time, studies will be made separately concerning a successor plane to the fighter-support fighters (F1).

(2) For strengthening and modernizing fire power, armored mobility and anti-tank fire power, tanks (including new-model tanks), guns, armored vehicles, and anti-tank firearms, including anti-boat and anti-tank guided missiles, launching devices, etc., will be consolidated. Efforts will be made to diversify the organization of divisions. At the same time, anti-tank helicopters (AH1S) will be consolidated to strengthen fire power from the air.

4. Transport Power and Mobility.

In order to strengthen transport power and mobility, transport planes (C-130H), transport helicopters (CH-47), etc., will be consolidated. Efforts will be made to consolidate transport ships.

5. Intelligence, Reconnaissance and Command/Communications Capabilities.

(1) In order to improve guard, surveillance and intelligence collection capabilities, the modernization of the Base Air Defense Ground Environment System and the consolidation of various intelligence-collection means will continue to be pushed. Also, in regard to over-the-horizon radar, its utility, etc., will be checked into separately and necessary measures will be taken.

(2) For strengthening air reconnaissance capability, a part of the interceptor-fighters (F4EJs) which our country now has, will be converted to reconnaissance planes.

(3) For the improvement of the command/communication capability, the modernization of the defense communication network will be pushed. At the same time, various other measures, such as the utilization of communication satellites, etc., will be promoted.

6. Immediate-Response Setup, Continuous Combat Capability and Sustainability.

(1) In order to improve the immediate-response setup, part of the tanks will be transferred and deployed in Hokkaido, and efforts will be made to improve the first stage coping capability in the region. At the same time, various measures, such as preparation of mines and torpedoes for immediate use, will be continued.

(2) In order to improve continuous-combat capability and sustainability, various measures, including the stockpiling of ammunition, the consolidation of air defense firearms at bases, and placing important facilities underground, will continue to be pushed.

7. Education and Training Systems and Rescue Setup.

In order to improve the education and training systems and the rescue mission, aircraft, training support ships, etc., will be consolidated, such as medium grade training planes (T-4s), rescue seaplanes (US1As), new type rescue helicopters, etc.

8. Personnel and Medical Care.

In order to secure the necessary personnel and to enhance esprit de corps, necessary personnel measures, such as the improvement of their treatment, etc., and medical care measures, will be promoted.

9. Facilities.

Facilities needed for the acquisition of equipment and the organization of units, etc., will be consolidated. Efforts will also be made to consolidate and improve the livelihood environment of the personnel and existing facilities, such as ammunition depots, training facilities, etc.

10. Technology Research and Development.

Research and development of a new anti-submarine helicopter (type to be carried on board ships) system, various types of guided missiles and other equipment and material will be promoted, and efforts will be made to improve technological research and development.

11. Support for the Stationing of U.S. Forces in Japan.

In order to contribute to the smooth and effective operation of the Japan-U.S. Security Treaty structure, various measures to support U.S. Forces in Japan will continue to be promoted.

12. Other.

(1) Studies concerning mid-air refueling functions, such as the performance of mid-air refueling planes, plans for their operation, etc., will be pushed.

(2) In order to improve on-the-sea air defense capability, studies will be made for an effective on-the-sea air defense system through the combination of various kinds of equipment.

III. Scale of Consolidation

See the attached chart

Comparison between the Attached Chart of "General Outline" and the New Plan

			Defense Plan General Outline (National Defense Program Outline - TAIKO)	FY1985 Completion Time	New Plan Completion Time
	Fixed Number of SDF Personnel		180,000 men	180,000	180,000
GSDF	Mainstay Units	Units to be deployed regionally in peacetime	12 divisions	12	12
			2 mixed brigades	2	2
		Mobile units	1 armored division	1	1
			1 artillery brigade	1	1
			1 airborne brigade	1	1
			1 instructors brigade	1	1
			1 helicopter brigade	1	1
		Low altitude air-defense surface-to-air guided missile units	8 anti-aircraft artillery units	8	8
MSDF	Mainstay Units	Anti-submarine surface ship units (task forces)	4 escort ship flotillas	4	4
		Anti-submarine surface ship units (regional)	10 units	10	10
		Submarine units	6 units	6	6
		Mine-sweeper units	2 mine-sweeper units	2	2
		Ground-based anti-submarine units	16 units	14	16
	Main equipment	Anti-submarine surface ships	About 60 ships	58	62
		Submarines	16 submarines	14	16
		Aircraft for operational use	About 220 planes	145	214
ASDF	Mainstay Units	Aircraft control and warning groups	28 control groups	28	28
		Interceptor-fighter units	10 flight squadrons	10	10
		Fighter-support fighter units	3 flight squadrons	3	3
		Air reconnaissance units	1 flight squadron	1	1
		Air transport units	3 flight squadrons	3	3
		Warning flight units	1 flight squadron	1	1
		High altitude air-defense surface-to-air guided missiles units	6 AA artillery groups	6	6
	Main equipment	Aircraft for operational use	About 430 planes	372	415

87

IV. Required Expenses

The upper limit of defense-related expenses, needed for the implementation of this plan, will generally aim at about 18.4 trillion yen, at prices in fiscal 1985. However, in the compilation of the budget for each fiscal year, efforts will be made for still greater efficiency and rationalization, and to hold down the expenditures as much as possible. At the same time, the budget for each fiscal year will be decided, taking into consideration the economic and financial circumstances at a given time and the recognition of the nation's various other measures.

V. Outlook for the Plan

This Plan will be reviewed as occasion demands, and after three years, a re-formulation, once again, will be made based on economic and financial circumstances, moves in the international situation, and technological trends.

Source: *Tokyo Shimbun*, September 19,1985.

Appendix E.
National Defense Program Outline

1. Objectives

Japan's possession of a defense capability within the scope permitted by the Constitution is not only a concrete expression of the people's will to safeguard the nation's peace and independence, but also aims - together with the Japan-United States security arrangement - directly at forestalling any aggression against Japan and repelling such aggression should it occur. Concurrently, the very fact that Japan firmly maintains such a defense posture contributes as well to the international political stability of Japan's neighboring region.

A major consideration in this regard is the nature of the defense capability which Japan should possess. Assuming that the international political structure in this region, along with continuing efforts for global stabilization, will not undergo any major changes for some time to come, and that Japan's domestic conditions will also remain fundamentally stable, the most appropriate defense goal would seem to be the maintenance of a full surveillance posture in peacetime and the ability to cope effectively with situations up to the point of limited and small-scale aggression. The emphasis is on the possession of the assorted functions required for national defense, while retaining balanced organization and deployment, including logistical support. At the same time, it is felt that consideration should be given to enabling this defense posture to contribute to the domestic welfare through disaster-relief operations and other such programs.

Japan has steadily improved its defense capability through the drafting and implementation of a series of four defense buildup plans. At this time, the present scale of defense capability seems to closely approach the target goals of the above mentioned concept.

This outline is meant to serve as a guideline for Japan's future defense posture in the light of that concept. Based on the information given below, efforts will be made to qualitatively maintain and improve defense capability, and fulfill the purpose of that capability, in specific upgrading, maintenance, and operation of defense functions.

2. International Situation

An analysis of the current international situation, at the time of drafting this outline, was made as follows:

During recent years, the world community has witnessed a pronounced trend toward more diversified international relations. While nationalistic movements have become more active in some countries, simultaneously there has been marked intensification of interdependence among nations.

Against this background, the major geopolitical blocs of East and West - which center on the relationship between the United States and the Soviet Union and their continued overwhelming military strengths - have continued a dialogue aimed at avoiding nuclear war and improving mutual relations, allowing for certain twists and turns along the path. In many individual regions as well, various efforts are being made to avoid conflict and stabilize international relations.

Deeply-rooted factors for assorted confrontations remain within the East-West relationship revolving around the United States and the Soviet Union, however, and intra-regional situations as well are fluid in many aspects with various elements of instability observable.

Within the general neighborhood of Japan, an equilibrium exists, involving the three major powers of the United States, the Soviet Union, and China. Tension still persists on the Korean Peninsula, however, and military buildups continue in several countries near Japan.

Under present circumstances, though, there seems little possibility of a full-scale military clash between East and West or of a major conflict possibly leading to such a clash, due to the military balance - and the various efforts being made to stabilize international relations.

Furthermore, while the possibility of limited military conflict breaking out in Japan's neighborhood cannot be dismissed, this equilibrium between the super powers and the existence of the Japan-U.S. security arrangement seems to play a major role in maintaining international stability, and in preventing full-scale aggression against Japan.

3. Basic Defense Concept

(1) Prevention of Armed Invasion

Japan's basic defense policy is to possess an adequate defense capability of its own while establishing a posture for the most effective operation of that capability to prevent aggression. In addition, a defense posture capable of dealing with any aggression should be constructed, through maintaining the credibility of the Japan-U.S. security arrangement and insuring the smooth functioning of that system.

Against nuclear threat, Japan will rely on the nuclear deterrent capability of the United States.

(2) Countering Aggression

Should indirect aggression - or any unlawful military activity which might lead to aggression against this nation - occur, Japan will take immediate responsive action in order to settle the situation at an early stage.

Should direct aggression occur, Japan will repel such aggression at the earliest possible stage by taking immediate responsive action and trying to conduct an integrated, systematic operation of its defense capability. Japan will repel limited and small-scale aggression, in principle without external assistance. In cases where the unassisted repelling of aggression is not feasible, due to scale, type or other factors of such aggression, Japan will continue an unyielding resistence by mobilizing all available forces until such time as cooperation from the United States is introduced, thus rebuffing such aggression.

4. Posture of National Defense

In accordance with the above defense concepts, Japan will maintain a defense capability of the postures spelled out below. This defense capability will meet the functional and postural requirements outlined in Section I as to what Japan should possess. At the same time, it will be standarized so that, when serious changes in situations so demand, the defense structure can be smoothly adapted to meet such changes.

(1) Setup of Warning and Surveillance

Japan's defense structure must possess continuous capability to conduct warning and surveillance missions within Japan's territory and neighboring seas and airspace as well as to collect required intelligence.

(2) Setup for Countering Indirect Aggression and Unlawful Actions by Means of Use of Military Power

(a) Japan's defense structure must possess the capability to act and take the required steps to respond to such cases as intense domestic insurgency with external support, organized personnel infiltration and arms

93

smuggling, or the covert use of force in Japan's nearby seas and airspace.

(b) Japan's defense structure must be capable of immediate and pertinent action to cope with aircraft invading or threatening to invade Japan's territorial airspace.

(3) Setup for Countering Direct Military Aggression

Japan's defense structure must be capable of taking immediate responsive action against any direct military aggression, in accordance with the type and scale of such aggression. It should be capable of repelling limited and small-scale aggression, in principle without external assistance. In cases where unassisted repelling of aggression is not feasible, it should be capable of continuing effective resistence until such time as cooperation from the United States can be introduced, thus rebuffing such aggression.

(4) Setup of Command Communications, Transportation and Rear Support Services

Japan's defense structure must be able to function in such fields as command communications, transportation, rescue, supply and maintenance, for swift, effective and adequate operations.

(5) Setup of Education and Training of Personnel

Japan's defense structure must be capable of carrying out intensive education and training of personnel at all times for the reinforcement of the personnel foundation of defense capability.

(6) Setup of Disaster-Relief Operations

Japan's defense structure must possess the capability to carry out disaster-relief operations in any areas of the country when required.

Realization of the structuring outlined below for the Ground, Maritime, and Air Self Defense Forces is a basic requirement for maintenance of the defense posture.

5. Posture of the Ground, Maritime, and Air Self Defense Forces

In addition, special consideration must be given to promoting systematic cooperation among the three branches of the SDF, and to securing maximum efficiency in integrated operations.

(1) Ground Self Defense Force

(a) The Ground Self Defense Force, in order to be capable of swift and effective systematic defense operations from the outset of aggression in any part of Japan, must deploy its divisions and other units with a balance conforming to Japan's natural features.

(b) The GSDF must possess at least one tactical unit of each of the various types of forces used mainly for mobile operations.

(c) The GSDF must possess ground-to-air missile units capable of undertaking low-altitude air defense of vital areas.

(2) Maritime Self Defense Force

(a) The MSDF must possess one fleet escort force as a mobile operating ship unit in order to quickly respond to aggressive action and such situations at sea. The fleet escort force must be able to maintain at least one escort flotilla on alert at all times.

(b) The MSDF must possess, as ship units assigned to coastal surveillance and defense, surface anti-submarine capability of at least one ship division in operational readiness at all times in each assigned sea district.

(c) The MSDF must maintain fixed-wing anti-submarine aircraft units in order to provide the capability of carrying out such missions as surveillance and patrol of the nearby seas and surface ship protection.

(3) Air Self Defense Force

(a) The Air Self Defense Force must possess aircraft control and warning units capable of vigilance and surveillance throughout Japanese airspace on a continuous basis.

(b) The ASDF must possess fighter units and high-altitude ground-to-air missile units for air defense, to provide the capability of maintaining continuous alert to take immediate and appropriate steps against violation of Japan's territorial airspace and air incursions.

(c) The ASDF must possess units capable of engaging in such missions as interdicting airborne or amphibious invasion, air support, aerial reconnaissance, early warning against low-altitude intrusion and air transportation as the necessity arises.

Descriptions of the actual scales of organizations and primary equipment under the foregoing concepts are given in the attachment.

6. Basic Policy and Matters to be Taken into Consideration in Building Up Defense Capabilities

The basic goal in improving Japan's defense capability must be the maintenance of the postures outlined above, with due consideration to qualitative improvements aimed at parity with the technical standards of other nations. In addition to carefully adapting to changing economic and fiscal conditions in harmony with government policies in other fields, the points below should be borne in mind when defense improvements are actually implemented.

Decisions on major projections in fiscal yearly defense improvement programs will be submitted to the National Defense Council for consultation. The actual scope of such major projections will be decided by the Cabinet, after consultation with the Nataional Defense Council.

(1) Establishment of reasonable standards for personnel recruitment and consideration of measures aimed at securing quality personnel and enhancing morale.

(2) Effective maintenance and improvement of defense facilities and attempts to harmonize such facilities with the surrounding communities through consideration of environmental protection, such as anti-noise measures.

(3) Effective implementation of equipment acquisition programs, with overall consideration of such factors as swift emergency resupply, acceptable education and training ease and cost efficiency. Attention should also be given to the possibility for adequate domestic production of the edquipment in question.

(4) Improvement of the technical research and development system for the maintenance and improvement of qualitative levels of defense capability.

<u>Self-Defense Personnel Quota</u>   <u>180,000 Men</u>

Basic Units
   Units deployed regionally in peacetime   12 Divisions
                                       2 Composite Brigades
GSDF   Mobile Operation Units   1 Armored Division
                                         1 Artillery Brigade
                                       1 Airborne Brigade
                                       1 Training Brigade
                                       1 Helicopter Brigade
   Low-Altitude Ground-to-Air Missile Units   8 Anti-Aircraft Artil
                                          Groups

Basic Units
  Anti-submarine Surface-Ship Units
   (for mobile operations)   4 Escort Flotillas
  Anti-submarine Surface Ship Units
  (Regional District Units)   10 Divisions
MSDF Submarine Units   6 Divisions
  Minesweeping Units   2 Flotillas
  Land-based Anti-submarine Aircraft Units   16 Squadrons

Main Equipment
  Anti-submarine Surface Ships   Apx. 60 Ships
  Submarines   16 Submarines
  Combat Aircraft   Apx. 220 Aircraft

Basic Units
  Aircraft Control and Warning Units   28 Groups
  Interceptor Units   10 Squadrons
ASDF Support Fighter Units   3 Squadrons
  Air Reconnaissance Units   1 Squadron
  Air Transport Units   3 Squadrons
  Early Warning Units   1 Squadron
  High-Altitude Ground-to-Air Missile Units   6 Groups

Main Equipment
  Combat Aircraft   Apx. 430 Aircraft

Note: This list is based upon the equipment structure that the SDF
     possesses, or is scheduled to possess, at the time of the
     drafting of this National Defense Program Outline.

Appendix F.

Conference on
Japanese Defense Policy

Role of the Bureaucrat and
Politician in Japanese
Security Management

Report of the Conference
Coordinator

Harrison Holland

Sponsored by
The Hoover Institution
Stanford University
Stanford, California

Conference held at
International House, Tokyo
December 4,1985

CONTENTS

Preface

Introduction

99

Preface

The Hoover Institution conducted a study of Japanese security management in 1985/86 concentrating on the principal institutions that influence the pace and shape of Japanese defense, the bureaucracy (Ministries of Finance, International Trade and Industry, Foreign Affairs, the Defense Agency, the Prime Minister's Office), the military establishment, the Diet, the media and research organizations and the defense industry. The study's objective was to analyze the role of each of these elements in developing Japanese defense policy in order to better understand how Japan manages its security. Such knowledge would help U.S. policymakers promote policies and programs that would hopefully lead to greater equity in defense burden-sharing between Japan and the United States in Northeast Asia.

The first conference on the role of the politician and the bureaucrat in Japanese security management is the subject of this report.

The basis for discussion at the December 4, 1985 meeting was a paper prepared by Professor Shin'ichi Kamata of the National Defense Academy, Yokosuka, Japan and Dr. Harrison Holland of the Hoover Institution and the Northeast Asia-United States Forum on International Pollicy at Stanford University which analyzed the role of the politician and the bureaucrat in the formation and implementation of the defense budget, the National Defense Program Outline (TAIKO) and the Mid-Term Planning Estimate (CHUGYO). The conference was an informal gathering of Japanese defense authorities representing the government, the Liberal Democratic Party, research organizations, the military services, the media and academia. The proceedings were conducted in the Japanese language and translated into English by Miss Kumie Kushizaki. A list of participants is at the end of this report.

The conference was divided into three sessions. The first session was devoted to a discussion of the defense budget including budget decision-making, the 1% of GNP problem, the issue of deferred payments and the influence of the United States on the budget process.

The second session examined the TAIKO and CHUGYO and their impact on the defense program, considered prospects for change in the TAIKO and CHUGYO and analyzed the influence of TAIKO on the problem of United States-Japan defense burden-sharing.

The final session was devoted to summing up the reaction of participants to the influence of the bureaucrat and politician in defense policy-making and to the impact of the defense budget, TAIKO and CHUGYO on Japanese security management. Each individual gave his own opinion on how U.S. policymakers could gain greater Japanese support for U.S.-Japan security relations and through such support and cooperation a more equitable sharing of defense burdens in the Western Pacific.

It is a pleasure to acknowledge the financial support given this conference by the Japan-United States Friendship Commission. Special thanks are due Mr. Tomohisa Sakanaka who moderated the first session and Mr. Keiichi Ito who presided over the second and third sessions. The ultimate success of any conference must depend on the quality of the participants . This conference was no exception. To the representatives of the Defense Agency, the Foreign Ministry, the media, academic institutions, the admirals and generals of the Self-Defense Forces, to the American Embassy, Tokyo, and to my colleagues in Japan and the United States, I am very grateful. I alone am responsible for any problems that arose during the conference and for this report.

Harrison Holland
Conference Coordinator

Introduction

United States-Japan security relations have long been uneven insofar as shared responsibility is concerned. The Security Treaty which is the cornerstone of these relations commits the United States to come to the defense of Japan in case of attack but does not require a similar commitment from the Japanese. Recently, the United States has pressed Japan to assume more responsibility for her own defense yet little progress has been made in reaching this goal.

In an effort to enhance defense cooperation and understanding between the two countries, the conference sought answers to such questions as why the Japanese are reluctant to do more to defend themselves, why they have mandated a slow, measured buildup of their military forces despite urgings of the United States for a greater defense effort and why the United States has been unable to substantially influence the scope and pace of the Japanese defense buildup.

The Kamata/Holland report given to each participant concluded that answers to these questions could be found in the constraints on Japanese defense policy that are inhibiting efforts of bureaucrats and politicians to improve Japan's defense capabilities. Chief among these constraints is the Constitution and its Article 9 which renounces war as an instrument of national policy. Other restraints are the National Defense Program Outline and its accompanying policy of limiting annual defense spending to 1% of the Gross National Product, concern over the reaction of Japan's neighbors to Japanese rearmament, a relatively weak Japanese Defense Agency that finds it difficult to compete bureaucratically with its chief adversary, the Ministry of Finance, an austere national budget that holds down most expenditures for programs, a markedly different perception of the threat from the Soviet Union than held by the United States - while concerned about the Soviet military buildup in the area, the public does not believe that the USSR has any intention of attacking Japan - and, perhaps most significantly, public opinion which although finally accepting the Self Defense Forces as necessary for the defense of Japan, nevertheless is concerned that the annual defense budget not exceed 1% of GNP and that Japan not proceed too fast in her military buildup. This cautious attitude is a mixture of concern about resurgent militarism, a strong belief in the sanctity of Article 9 of the Constitution and a reluctance to spend more than the minimum necessary to insure continued support by the United States for Japanese security.

Testing the validity of these conclusions was the main task of conference participants. They not only addressed these conclusions but studied the influence and responsibilities of the bureaucrat and politician in defense policy decision-making and the institutional and managerial factors that bear on the ability of these individuals to formulate national defense policy and manage the defense establishment.

The conversations were lively, frank by ordinary Japanese standards and revealed the strong emotions associated with the defense debate in Japan. Some disagreed with the general findings, others agreed, some chose to mute criticism, others to emphasize certain aspects of the problem at the expense of frontal attacks on the main questions raised in the report. Most participants expressed satisfaction at the opportunity to trade views and opinions with their contemporaries and left the conference with a feeling that they had had a chance to vent their frustrations and say what was on their minds. The report which follows will give an indication of the mood of the participants, their reaction to the central findings of the report and their hopes and advice on how Japan's defense effort should progress.

The Kamata/Holland report was based on the premise that a study of the defense budget process, the National Defense Program Outline and the Mid-Term Planning Estimate would provide valuable clues on the scope and level of influence wielded by the bureaucrat and politician in Japanese security management.

The paper gave conference participants an overview of defense organization and highlighted the key bureaucratic elements in the Defense Agency, the Constitution and laws that provide the legal framework for defense policy, and the operation of the National Defense Council, the Diet and the Prime Minister's Office.

Attention then focused on a study of the decision-making process and how participants in the process negotiated and maneuvered within their sphere of influence to shape the size and content of the defense budget. Budget strategy was discussed along with the roles of key Finance Ministry and Defense Agency bureaucrats, Diet committees and the opposition political parties.

The impact of the 1% ceiling on the defense buildup was examined along with the influence of the National Defense Program Outline and the Mid-Term Planning Estimate on defense policy.

The paper concluded with a series of policy recommendations and invited comments from conference participants on these recommendations.

During the first session, conference members made clear their belief that the defense budget was not meeting the security needs of Japan and that the 1% ceiling policy was chiefly to blame. A key Liberal Democratic Party member, Shiina, Motoo who was invited to the conference but was unable to attend because of a previous commitment, told Kamata and Holland in a separate interview that the 1% ceiling on defense spending should be removed; that the Japanese people should receive more guidance from the government on key defense issues and that politicians should play a more decisive role in defense policy. He thought that this was beginning to happen and that bureaucrats were increasingly deferring to politicians in the defense debate, largely because of American pressure on Japan to do more in her defense buildup program. As politicians are mainly responsible for basic foreign policy decisions that affect U.S.-Japan relations, it was natural, thought Shiina, that politicians assume a more dominant role.

Several participants criticized politicians and bureaucrats for not exerting the leadership necessary to enhance Japan's defense capability but acknowledged that at least for the politicians it was difficult to do because of the political risks involved. Deferred payments or the policy of "buy now and pay later" was cited as an example of inexcusable bureaucratic intrusion into defense policy by the Finance Ministry which has resulted in the Defense Agency annually sinking deeper into debt. The military participants were especially provoked at politicians for not exerting the influence necessary to stem the budget hemorrhage caused by deferred payments.

The United States was faulted by several participants for inconsistency in defense policy vis-a-vis Japan. This lack of policy consonance is causing confusion among defense planners in Tokyo on what course Japan is expected to follow in her security relations with the United States.

One member of the conference, Natsume Haruo, former Vice Minister of the Defense Agency, stressed the importance of a new approach to U.S.-Japan security relations. He suggested that the Security Treaty between the two countries be re-studied to bring greater balance into the relationship. It is time, he thought, for Japan to assume more responsibility under the Treaty. While some participants agreed with Natsume, they noted that the controversiality of the defense issue in Japanese politics makes it very difficult for political leaders to undertake a reassessment of defense relations with the United States.

The second session was devoted to a discussion of the TAIKO and CHUGYO and it was soon apparent that most participants believed that TAIKO had outlived its usefulness, was not meeting present security needs, and was ill-fitted to deal with military emergencies. TAIKO was established in 1976 at a time when the public was becoming increasingly uneasy over defense spending and detente was having a lulling effect on the public mood. To gain public consensus on the defense issue and defuse mounting public skepticism over defense policy, TAIKO was conceived as the instrument to create better public understanding on defense, to calm Japanese agitation over the defense budget and to re-direct defense programs toward a more peaceful image of the Self Defense Forces. It worked, and for ten years thereafter, TAIKO has been the charter for the defense buildup, emphasizing weapons procurement over a conceptual approach to defense policy. But today, as several participants noted, the international environment has changed, Japan has become a major economic force in the world and her new economic power requires that she undertake more responsibility for her own defense. Participants debated the pros and cons of modifying TAIKO, abolishing it, or leaving it as is. Most concluded that the present political climate was not conducive to change; that the public would not stand for it and that politicians, especially leaders of the Liberal Democratic Party, were unwilling to take the political risks involved in changing TAIKO.

Several members believed that the new 5-year plan, which has now taken the place of CHUGYO and has been elevated to a national policy, could result in a "fading away" of TAIKO and conceivably the abolition of the 1% ceiling on the defense budget. Some felt that the new 5-year plan was a clever move by Mr. Nakasone to accomplish these objectives. Others were not so sure and thought that both TAIKO and the new 5-year plan would form the core of Japanese defense policy for the next 5 years. While speculating on the point, all participants were nevertheless convinced that TAIKO was no longer providing the necessary guidance for Japan's defense policy. Yet they thought that to change TAIKO at this juncture would require more political courage than was presently evident in Japan's political leadership.

The last session dealt with comments of members on the recommendations contained in the Kamata/Holland draft advocating closer working relations on defense between the two countries. More effective collaboration, the paper contended, would deepen understanding of the mutual problems faced by the two countries in security management, would cause more light to be shed on the roles of bureaucrats and politicians in defense policy and would hopefully move Japanese leaders to play a more responsible role in directing Japanese security policy toward greater cooperation and equity in burden-sharing between Japan and the United States.

All participants agreed in principle that better understanding was important, that closer contact between various groups having responsibility for shaping and carrying out defense policies in both countries was desirable and could lead to more effective cooperation. Developing joint defense plans and establishing common security goals were essential. But to move in a positive way toward these objectives required a reevaluation of the security relationship in light of changing international conditions and particularly because of the growing Soviet military presence in Northeast Asia.

There was unanimity that a better climate for cooperation could be advanced by quiet diplomacy rather than loud complaints and public badgering of Japan to do more in her defense buildup program.

At the close of the conference, all members expressed satisfaction with the discussions and voiced the hope that similar exchanges among Japanese experts on defense matters could lead to a greater consensus on the defense issue in Japan. For consensus, they felt, was critical if Japan is to move forward to meet the challenges of the latter part of this decade.

Session I

The Defense Budget
A. Decision-making:
the politician and
the bureaucrat
B. The 1% Problem
C. Deferred Payments
D. U.S. Influence

A. Decision-making

The defense budget is subject to a process that begins in April and lasts through December. Involved are military officers from the three services, key officials in the powerful internal bureaus of the Defense Agency, officials of the Finance Ministry's budget bureau, officers in the ministries of International Trade and Industry and Foreign Affairs, important members of the Secretariat of the National Defense Council, key defense and policy committees of the ruling Liberal Democratic Party, and ultimately the Prime Minister, certain Cabinet members and senior faction leaders of the Liberal Democratic Party. *Nemawashi* (behind-the-scenes manuevering) and *ringisei* (consensus building) are the principal methods by which spending levels are set and procurement decisions made. Most controversy centers on the 15 to 20% of the budget earmarked for procurement of weapons systems. Entitlement costs comprise the great bulk of the defense budget, salaries and logistical support.

Sakanaka suggested that the power of civilian officials in the Defense Agency greatly exceeds that of military personnel. He stressed that the responsibilities of civilian and military officials were quite different; that different functions required different levels of expertise. He believed that while frictions exist between the Defense Agency and other ministries, especially with the Finance Ministry, seconded officials from other ministries occupying powerful positions in the Internal Bureaus of the Defense Agency (*naikyoku*) bring a broader vision to the security problems facing Japan. This is good for Japan and good for the Defense Agency.

Sakanaka said that to appreciate the roles of the Finance Ministry and the Defense Agency in budget decision-making, it is important to understand that the Ministry has responsibility for allocating resources among all government ministries and agencies whereas the Defense Agency is concerned only with obtaining funds for the three military services and other related departments of the defense establishment. Conflicts are thus inevitable given the differences in responsibilities.

Sakanaka also took issue with those who contend that if pressure is applied to one or several key officials in the defense budget process, results favorable to the Defense Agency would occur. He thought that this was simplistic reasoning and did not recognize the importance of nemawashi and ringisei in the decision-making process.

Masuzoe took a slightly different tack. He questioned whether the kacho (division chief) has as much power in the decision-making process as some studies have suggested. He said that his research has shown that during the

107

nemawashi and *ringisei* process, the kacho seldom ventures beyond his own bureaucratic level in meetings with officials and politicians to discuss budget problems. He thought their liaison function more critical to the budget process than the inherent power of their position.

Nishihara believed that the term civilian control to describe the budget process implied that civilian officials of the *naikyoku* supressed the thoughts and actions of uniformed personnel. He admitted that this notion was held by many Japanese, but he felt it more important to view civilian control in the broader context of military personnel being subordinated to the political leadership of Japan rather than in the narrower sense of military-civilian relations in the Defense Agency.

Nishihara also took exception to the statement by some Japanese commentators and mentioned in the Kamata/Holland report that the National Defense Council (NDC) was merely a "rubber stamp" for budget decisions. He thought the reality quite different. He noted that within the NDC, especially the NDC Secretariat, considerable discussion takes place on defense policy, budget allocations and CHUGYO estimates. He also stressed that the Prime Minister and the Director General of the Defense Agency play a significant role in the budget decision-making process. He believed that the Foreign Ministry, especially the North American Affairs Bureau of the ministry, is not an "invisible force" in defense policy as the Kamata/Holland report suggested, but plays a significant role in bringing to bear foreign policy implications of defense budget decisions. He also felt that more emphasis needed to be put on the positive and negative pressures emanating from within the factions of the *yato* (opposition political parties) and *yoto* (the ruling Liberal Democratic Party) on defense policy.

Ito had a somewhat different view of the role of the NDC in the decision-making process.He acknowledged that the NDC was a rather weak link in the process. He said this was due mainly to the inability of NDC members to devote enough time to their responsibilities as NDC officials. Most of the key members are Cabinet Ministers, are generally in those positions for a year or less, must devote most of their time to their own ministry responsibilities and thus have little time left for the NDC. The main responsibility for NDC decision-making thus falls on members of the Secretariat of the NDC. Even these officials have other duties in their own ministries so the net result is that important decisions on the budget are made outside the NDC. Ito implied that rivalry existed between the *naikyoku* and the Secretariat of the NDC and the relative power of the two institutions could often be measured by the strong leadership evident in each organization. He noted that during the tenure of Kaihara and Kubo, both energetic leaders, the *naikyoku* dominated debate on the budget and other defense policies. He thought that the relationship between the NDC Secretariat and the *naikyoku* could profit from study and possible administrative reform.

Retired Admiral Kitamura tended to resent the domination of the *naikyoku* in military affairs and was especially critical of the Finance Ministry for excessive interference in the details of military procurement. Civilian control and the domination of the *naikyoku* in military affairs limit the ability of the military to carryout their responsibilities. The yato is always opposed to the military and to the defense budget and the yoto gives only half-hearted support to the military. The politicians and bureaucrats that do support the Defense Agency and the Self Defense Forces are often subject to criticism in Diet debates and by the media. This is the reality of civilian control of the defense establishment and it is not right.

Onishi focused on the role of the Ministry of International Trade and

Industry (MITI) and the Foreign Ministry by commenting that MITI had played a rather insignificant role in the defense budget process whereas the Foreign Ministry has given more meaning and brought greater understanding to the foreign policy implications of defense budget decisions.

Retired Admiral Yoshida sought to play down the importance of friction between the military and the *naikyoku*, stating that each has its own responsibilities and must be so judged. The *naikyoku* deals with the political realities of defense policy whereas the military must stick to the job of improving the capability of the Self Defense Forces to defend Japan through joint training and planning with United States forces in Japan.

Kato prefaced his remarks by noting that inasmuch as he was presently the chief of the Legal Division of the Treaties Bureau of the Foreign Ministry, his comments were his own and did not necessarily reflect the views of the Foreign Ministry. He took some pains to explain the role of the division chief in the budget process, at times taking issue with Masuzoe over the power of the kacho in budget deliberations. He acknowledged the strength of the Finance Ministry in budget negotiations and pointed out that the degree of effectiveness of the kacho is often related to his physical strength. Long, tedious negotiations tend to deplete the energies of the kacho and unless he is backed by a strong staff, as is often the case in the Finance Ministry, he loses some of his effectiveness. He also said that Japanese domestic laws sometimes limit the ability of the Defense Agency to work with United States forces in Japan.

Takubo thought that rivalry among the three military services was harmful to Japan's defense effort and penalized the Self Defense Forces in the budget process. He also agreed with Kitamura that the Finance Ministry dominates the Defense Agency in defense budget decision-making.

Kitamura concurred that rivalry existed among the three services; that each has a different view of its responsibilities for the defense of Japan. As Kitamura saw it, the Ground Self Defense Forces protect the land, the Air Self Defense Forces the sky over Japan, but the Maritime Self Defense Forces must contend with the oceans that surround Japan. It is important, he believed, that this point be considered in negotiations over the budget and broader defense policies.

Ito explained that the growth of the defense budget has been limited because Japan was devoting more of its resources to social welfare. Once the priority was established during the Fukuda administration to give preference to welfare over defense in the national budget, the Defense Agency was reluctant to challenge the policy and this accounted for the slow growth in defense spending.

On a related subject, Masuzoe claimed that it was inaccurate to compare the defense budget process to a kabuki play as suggested in the Kamata/Holland report. The defense budget is the product of long and careful negotiations, he said, where the outcome is not always predictable. And the Prime Minister, he contended, is not always the decisive voice in the process. He must exert his leadership while confronting a never-ending factional power struggle within the ruling Liberal Democratic Party. Few Prime Ministers, except for Mr. Nakasone, have been able or have wanted to make an issue with the party over increase defense spending. Even Nakasone has failed, for example, to gain yoto support for eliminating the 1% ceiling on the defense budget.

Retired Admiral Yoshida blamed politics for the inadequate defense budget. He said that despite long and detailed negotiations between the *naikyoku* and the three military services that produced budget recommendations considered appropriate to support defense policy, the defense budget allocation was still too small. As a result, the TAIKO goal of 40% achievement was only running at about 27% and this was due directly to a lack of adequate funding. He believed that the media was giving the public the wrong picture of defense, especially at a time when the United States has been urging Japan to do more to defend the homeland. Public opinion, nurtured by the media, has created problems for politicians at the very time Japan should be assuming more of the burden for her own defense. Politicians are unwilling to exert strong leadership on the defense question because of lukewarm public support for rearmament.

Kitamura supported Yoshida's general thesis. He thought that present defense budget difficulties are the result of yoto timidity. If the yoto had allocated more money for defense at a time of rapid economic expansion, there would not be the difficulties being experienced today in defense policy. He believed that the Japanese people are generally satisfied with the status quo, lulled by the American commitment to defend Japan under the U.S.-Japan Security Treaty. The Defense Agency should not worry unduly about attacks from the media. Newspapers will always criticize rearmament regardless of what the Defense Agency does. He thought the reality of the Soviet threat should get greater publicity; that the Defense Agency and top yoto leaders should begin a campaign to awaken the Japanese people to the threat to Japan's security. B.The

B.1% of GNP Problem

Many defense authorities attribute present budget difficulties to the decision of the Miki Cabinet in 1976 to limit annual defense spending to 1% of the Gross National Product. While this policy has put severe limitations on the Defense Agency, Japan's annual economic growth rate of between 3 and 6% has made it possible to increase defense spending and still remain within the 1% ceiling. But this policy has not set well with pro-defense groups. When the 1% issue was raised in this conference, several participants had harsh words for politicians whom they blamed for hobbling the defense effort.

Takubo welcomed Prime Minister Nakasone's efforts to remove the 1% ceiling and blamed Fukuda, Suzuki, Miki and former Defense Agency Director General Akagi for frustrating the Prime Minister's wishes. Political timidity is hurting Japan's defense buildup, according to Takubo, and creating unnecessary trouble for defense planners. The problem, Takubo thought, is that the public believes that removal of the 1% ceiling will return Japan to pre-war militarism. The blame for this public attitude, said Takubo, rests squarely with the Asahi, Mainichi and Tokyo newspapers. These papers constantly editorialize that abolishing the 1% barrier means a return to militarism and the politicians are listening. This explains why yoto leaders are unwilling to support Nakasone on the 1% issue.

Nishihara agreed with Takubo but took a different tack in explaining about the 1% problem. He thought that if the threat to Japan's security was clearly discernible to the public, the Japanese people would not object to an increase in defense spending. But even under these circumstances, the public would take refuge behind the American nuclear shield and people would comfort themselves with the knowledge that the United States would ultimately come to Japan's defense if attacked. This public attitude, said Nishihara, could be attributed to the concept of amae or dependency on the United States. This amae feeling shelters the Japanese people from the reality of the threat and makes it easier for them to oppose the elimination of the 1% ceiling.

Kato thought that one of the severe disadvantages of the 1% policy is that it tends to eliminate realistic debate on the defense program. For example, if the budget is kept within the 1% limit, people believe that all necessary defense requirements will be met. Yet they worry that if it exceeds 1% Japan will become remilitarized. This is unrealistic and leads to confused thinking. Under the present defense spending program, the emphasis is on the purchase of new weapons systems while the housing, training and welfare of Self Defense Force personnel are being neglected. This leads to low morale.

Ito suggested that blame for the 1% policy rests primarily with officials of the Defense Agency. In 1976 they were too anxious to agree to the Miki Cabinet policy on 1% and were unable to foresee the damage that the policy would do to Japanese defense policy.

Masuzoe thought that the 1% issue has become a political problem because of a lack of public consensus on defense. Thus the debate over 1% is not only a restraining factor on the Japanese Government leadership, but exercises a negative political hold on yoto leaders which is damaging to the defense effort.

Kato returned to the argument by suggesting that the United States simply did not understand the reasoning behind the 1% issue; that now that the U.S.-Japan relationship is on a more equal basis, the United States expects Japan to do its part and cannot understand why the 1% issue has become so ingrained in domestic Japanese politics. The 1% issue is also, quite unfortunately, having a rather negative impact on the trade problem between the two countries. The oyabun/kobun relationship (leader-follower), said Kato, is no longer a reality although it still seems to have some substance in the minds of Japanese. Despite this, Japan must assume more responsibility for her own defense and do a better job of helping the United States understand Japan's 1% predicament.

C. Deferred Payments

Deferred payments or "buy now and pay later" is becoming a critical problem for defense budget planners. Because of the 1% ceiling policy which has been in effect for the past 10 years together with the recent austere national budget, the Defense Agency, under Finance Ministry pressure, has had to limit the amount of downpayment for frontline equipment and increase the annual allocation for deferred payments at the expense of other defense programs involving logistical support activities, housing, training and welfare of Self Defense Force personnel. For example, in FY 1984, the Defense Agency contracted for over $6 billion of military equipment but put a little over $100 million as a downpayment. This lopsided ratio of downpayment to purchase price is causing the Defense Agency to annually slip deeper into debt. There seems no ready solution unless the defense budget is increased or equipment purchases cutback.

Sakanaka was alarmed over the growing Defense Agency debt. The "buy now and pay later" philosophy which is at the heart of the deferred payment problem is causing the Defense Agency to have to allocate more funds each year to pay off the mounting debt, often at the expense of acquiring important weapons systems and improving the morale of Self Defense Force personnel. The annual amount which must be taken from the overall defense budget to apply to deferred payments is generally negotiated between the *naikyoku* and the Finance Ministry in a way that is sheltered from public view. Sakanaka was worried that negotiations over how much to allocate to deferred payments would introduce an element of inflexibility into the defense procurement system. This could be especially harmful, he thought, to Japan's defense effort in time of emergency.

Ito believed that if the deferred payment problem was allowed to grow, it might become increasingly difficult to negotiate a realistic defense budget.

Natsume countered that the defense budget is adequate although the deferred payment problem might eventually cause some inflexibility in defense budget management. However, he thought that as deferred payments increase each year, the defense budget in its totality must increase in order that entitlement expenditures and weapons procurement can keep in step with a realistic defense program. These are the considerations that are at the heart of budget negotiations between the Finance Ministry and the Defense Agency. The austere national budget of recent years had complicated the defense budget picture and has given the Finance Ministry an opportunity to pressure the Defense Agency over the deferred payments issue, often reducing the amount that can be applied as a compromise for the Agency's desire to buy new weapons. In order to obtain the military hardware considered necessary for the defense of Japan, the Defense Agency has had to agree to Finance Ministry decisions over deferred payments. It is unfortunate, said Natsume, that this has had to happen, as it has caused the Defense Agency to slip further into debt. But under the tight national budget and given the 1% policy, the Defense Agency has had little choice but to go along with the Finance Ministry.

D.Influence of the United States on the Defense Budget

Pressure from the United States has helped those Japanese who advocate a more substantial buildup of Japan's defense forces. But the security relationship between the two countries remains unbalanced and voices are beginning to be heard within the Liberal Democratic Party and in defense circles for a re-examination of the relationship, to make it more equal. The task is a formidable one because of the continuing controversiality of the defense issue in Japanese politics. Japanese are often troubled by swings in U.S. policy and become confused and uncertain about what role Washington expects Japan to take in the security partnership. Greater consistency by the United States would enhance the effectiveness of American pressure. And, finally, closer consultation on a variety of international issues that affect the common security interests of Japan and the United States would produce a more knowledgeable Japanese leadership and perhaps a greater willingness on its part to be more open and forthright with the Japanese public on the need for more equality in the defense relationship between the two countries.

Masuzoe led off the discussion by pointing to American expectation of what Japan should be doing to defend herself. The United States must understand, he said, the domestic constraints under which Japanese defense policy is made; that Japan can only do so much given its defense budget; that the government must reassure the American public that Japan is doing all that can reasonably be expected. Masuzoe believed that the Japanese people lacked a realistic sense of the threat to their security and depended too much on the United States. He argued that as long as America is committed to protect Japan from the Soviet threat, current defense spending under the 1% policy is considered by most Japanese to be adequate. Some Japanese, he thought, believed that the United States was pressuring Japan to spend more on defense in order to persuade the Japanese to be more forthcoming on the trade issue. America's intention, as Masuzoe described it, was not to have Japan spend more money to protect herself, but to increase the defense budget in order to weaken Japan economically. In this way, he thought, the trade and defense issues become linked. Defense spending is a political device in Japan to deal with larger problems in U.S.-Japan relations.

Natsume believed that the time has come to take a new look at the U.S.-Japan Security Treaty; to adopt measures that would bring more balance into Japan's security relations with the United States. By limiting Japan's defense effort, said Natsume, the security relationship will remain unbalanced. It is time that Japan better appreciate the close security relations that exist with the United States and begin to consider how these relations could become more effective.

Ito said that when he was in the Defense Agency and had occasion to meet with American Congressmen, he got the impression that these Congressmen thought Japan was more interested in making profits than in protecting herself through realistic defense policies. Such Congressional reasoning produced demands that Japan spend more for her own defense.

Takubo thought there was little unanimity in American opinion on the Japanese defense issue. While Republicans demand that Japan do more to increase her defense capability, the Democrats would probably view such a development as an eventual threat to American security. This inconsistency in American opinion, as Takubo described it, has produced swings in American policy from pressuring Japan for a greater defense effort to expressing satisfaction with the status quo. This has caused confusion in Japanese government circles and uncertainty over American defense policy toward Japan. Unless American opinion can become consistent in its attitudes toward Japanese defense policy, exerting pressure will do little good. Such American inconsistency has given those in Japan wishing to eliminate the 1% ceiling, problems in gaining support for their position.

Kitamura opined that he was confused over American opinion regarding Japan's defense posture.One school in the United States feared that Japan would return to pre-war militarism while another group felt that Japan was not doing enough to build up her defense power. Meanwhile the Japanese Government was using the reported concerns of ASEAN countries over Japan's military buildup as an excuse to keep defense expenditures to a minimum. If the United States is genuinely interested in seeing Japan improve her defense capability, said Kitamura, the United States should help to persuade ASEAN countries that they have nothing to worry about from Japan's defense buildup program.

The National Defense Program
Outline (TAIKO) and the
Mid-Term Planning Estimate
(CHUGYO)

TAIKO

TAIKO was established in 1976 when domestic and international conditions were quite different from today (1986). Then the Japanese people were nervous over the amount of money spent for defense and worried that a rapid buildup of the Self Defense Forces might lead to militarism. A national consensus on defense policy was lacking. It was a time when some spoke of detente and a period when American military power was a source of assurance to the Japanese public.

Today Japan is faced with growing Soviet military strength on her doorstep, a relative decline in U.S. military power and a TAIKO that stresses the "peaceful" purpose of the Self Defense Forces, a philosophy that has frustrated Japanese defense planners in their efforts to cope with present day security realities.

TAIKO is essentially a guide for procurement of weapons, setting annual targets for the purchase of military equipment. Quantitative judgments take precedence over qualitative considerations in the TAIKO defense blueprint. TAIKO is considered the charter for national defense policy but it lacks a conceptual framework that would allow for broad strategies to meet the Soviet threat. It needs to be modified or re-interpreted but there is little interest in doing so within the ruling Liberal Democratic Party. The subject is too politically controversial.

Its companion, CHUGYO, was until September 1985 a purely internal planning instrument of the Defense Agency to allow for procurement decisions based upon current domestic and international conditions. CHUGYO judgments were made within the broad framework of TAIKO. In September 1985, Prime Minister Nakasone was able to get the CHUGYO or what is now known as the new 5-year plan elevated to a national policy. The new 5-year plan (1986-1990) is based upon the last CHUGYO and was established to breathe new life into the defense buildup program. However, like its predecessor and its parent TAIKO, the new 5-year plan lacks a conceptual vision which would allow, military equipment purchases to be more effectively related to policy needs. Some Japanese commentators suggest that the new 5-year plan may eventually take the place of TAIKO but the probability of this happening in the near future appears dim. It is more likely that the new plan, if administered carefully and with due regard to public concerns about defense spending, could be the vehicle for abolishing the 1% ceiling on defense spending.

Conference participants had mixed reactions to TAIKO and CHUGYO but a common thread running through most of their comments was that domestic and international conditions have changed substantially in the past 10 years and ways must be found either to gain greater flexibility in the interpretation of TAIKO guidelines or modify TAIKO to conform to present day realities.

Sakanaka led off the discussion by noting that TAIKO was established more to gain a national consensus on defense policy and increase the public's understanding of the military rather than as a response to detente. One result was to place a brake on defense spending. TAIKO focused mainly on the problem of defense equipment procurement rather than on broader conceptual considerations of defense policy.

Natsume agreed that domestic considerations outweighed international factors in establishing TAIKO. He said that during the 1960s and early 1970s when Japan's economy was expanding at a very healthy rate, defense spending was also rising and people began to worry about how much was being spent on the military. Meanwhile Defense Agency planners were purchasing frontline equipment at the expense of training and logistical support for military personnel. TAIKO was framed around the central idea of a "peaceful" military force that was not expected to have to deal with heavy attacks against Japan. It was devised as a politically strategic move to quiet public fears over excessive military spending. It gained the support of yato as well as important elements of yoto. Natsume stressed that international considerations were not the principal motivation for TAIKO. He noted further that domestic and international conditions have changed and TAIKO is no longer relevant as a prime guiding force for defense policy. TAIKO is so vague that many different policies can be justified under its umbrella. It thus allows yato opinions to clash with pro-defense views with the result that clear, objective defense policy determinations are lacking.

Natsume also opined that unless the direction of defense thinking in Japan changes, U.S.-Japan security relations will not achieve the necessary degree of understanding and mutual cooperation. Close cooperation between the United States and Japan is the best insurance policy for Japanese security. Japan must be able to respond to U.S. requests for cooperation and assume her responsibilities as a major member of the free world. TAIKO makes it difficult to do so. Yet to change TAIKO to allow for more flexibility in defense policy would be too politically controversial. Officials who suggest changes in TAIKO are often accused of advocating militarism. This inevitably arouses opposition. Natsume thought that the present Nakasone government was trying to gain support for a re-interpretation of TAIKO but without much success.

Kato said that TAIKO did not provide the flexibility for Japan to deal effectively with military emergencies. It is important for Japan to understand what the United States is saying about U.S.-Japan security relations. The Reagan administration's voice might in one instance be directed to the Congress, at another time to Japan and a third time to the U.S. public. Japan must be able to discern the difference. Also Japan should consider carefully the true nature of U.S.-U.S.S.R relations because shifts occur in these relations that could affect U.S.-Japan security policy. TAIKO does not allow for the Japanese Government to exercise its discretion in dealing with complex international and domestic conditions affecting Japanese security. But he doubted that TAIKO could be substantially changed because of strong yato opposition and the public's concern about militarism.

Masuzoe contended that it would be difficult to change TAIKO. Inasmuch as TAIKO was established on the basis of domestic concerns, any argument that TAIKO should be changed or modified on the basis of changes in U.S.-U.S.S.R relations, would be difficult to sell to the Japanese people. The relationship of TAIKO to the era of detente is especially troublesome for officials who wish to see TAIKO changed or abolished. Any return to an atmosphere of detente between the superpowers would make it increasingly difficult for the Japanese Government to do anything about TAIKO, especially given the secure feeling that would likely emerge in the public mind as a result of relaxed tensions between the United States and the Soviet Union.There is very little incentive in scholarly or other circles to educate the public on the realities of defense. It remains too controversial. Masuzoe reiterated what other participants said that TAIKO was too inflexible to meet the present needs of Japanese security.

Onishi stated that because world conditions have changed since TAIKO's inception in 1976, serious consideration must be given to meeting new circumstances. One problem for the Japanese is growing doubt about the credibility of the U.S.-Japan security system. The perception of the American commitment to defend free countries has changed, prompted in part, by U.S. demands that Japan do more to share the defense burden. Such a burden-sharing appeal was not heard at the time of TAIKO's formation; then the public and Japan's leaders felt confident that the U.S.-Japan Security Treaty would protect Japan. The problem of burden-sharing thus becomes linked to the issue of modifying TAIKO to meet the realities of the late 1980s.

Takubo was emphatic in advocating re-writing TAIKO although he was not optimistic that it would be possible. It was foolish to base TAIKO on detente. Even before TAIKO was established, President Ford, in April 1976, thought it better in discussing world affairs, to eliminate any reference to detente. So why was detente used as one justification for TAIKO? Inasmuch as the basic philosophy and assumptions underlying TAIKO were flawed, TAIKO could not then and still cannot today be a realistic policy for Japan's defense. He reminded his listeners that Japan is a leading world economic power but is not carrying her share of responsibility commensurate with her big power status. The political logic inside Japan regarding TAIKO is out of step with outside reality. Somehow both should come into balance. But TAIKO in its present form makes such a development extremely difficult. Domestic and international conditions that were present at the time of TAIKO's inauguration have changed. So must TAIKO.

Ito observed that it will not be easy to change TAIKO. It is, of course, necessary to improve the quality of Japan's military forces but TAIKO makes little provision for such a policy. Ito explained how difficult it was to discuss TAIKO with Liberal Democratic Party officials and opposition Socialist Party members because both sides have been debating the defense issue for years on the bases of different concepts and philosophies. However, in 1976, the yato and yoto sensing the need for consensus and for assuaging public concerns about the growing defense budget, supported the establishment of TAIKO. Times and conditions have changed and deep splits have developed between the opposition and the Liberal Democratic Party, differences that have always basically been there but were muted by the political realities of 1976. This is one reason why changing TAIKO today would be so difficult.

Ito also raised the point that America's present criticism of TAIKO is quite a change from the U.S. position in 1976 when TAIKO was supported in the belief that the new policy would enhance Japan's defense efforts. Continued debates in the United States and Japan over Japan's defense policy are meaningless, are contributing to the frustration of defense officials and making them more determined in their advocacy of change not only in the defense structure but in certain aspects of the Constitution as well. While many Defense Agency officials feel this way, Ito thought they could not realistically expect much change given the public mood and the different positions of the yato and yoto on defense.

Nishihara explained that TAIKO was based on a reliance on U.S. power to protect Japan and on a Self Defense Force that would deal only with limited or small-scale attacks. Now that the balance of power in Northeast Asia is slowly shifting toward the Soviet Union, TAIKO does not provide realistic guidance. Furthermore, in 1976, Japan's economy was just beginning to take off and it was logical from a domestic point of view to limit the size of the military forces. But now Japan is a strong economic power and it is illogical to expect her to continue to support a 1976-size Self Defense Force. Inasmuch as it would be very difficult, in Nishihara's opinion, to rewrite TAIKO, the next best thing would be to explain more fully the strategic policy based upon the goals of TAIKO.

In conclusion Nishihara stated with a good deal of emphasis that while the United States and Japan should cooperate in dealing with security problems, the strategic interests of the two countries do not necessarily always coincide. Japan should not depend so much on the United States. Japan should exercise more independence in her foreign policy. While it is sometimes hard to differentiate the strategic interests of Japan and the United States, it should be remembered that countries that are close neighbors of the Soviet Union may have a different point of view regarding their basic security interests from those that are not in close proximity to the U.S.S.R.

Kitamura joined those who advocated a change in TAIKO. He welcomed Nakasone's efforts to do something about TAIKO but felt that without the strong support of leaders of the Liberal Democratic Party, little could be accomplished. Certainly the Defense Agency could not do the job alone. He stressed that TAIKO was an obstacle to developing a militarily effective Self Defense Force. He noted strongly that while TAIKO was developed largely out of considerations of domestic politics, the international situation has now changed drastically with the development of Soviet SS 20 aimed at Japan and growing Russian military strength in Japan's backyard. There must be new thinking in the debate over Japan's security interests. It is necessary for politicians to recognize the serious threat to Japan's security, said Kitamura, but he was pessimistic that they would take necessary action to buildup Japan's defenses. He stressed that because of the growing Soviet threat, Japan's leaders would have to change their fundamental attitude about defense. TAIKO has become obsolete and is a hindrance to effective U.S.-Japan security cooperation in meeting the Soviet threat.

Nagano sided with those who believed that TAIKO had outlived its usefulness. He said that the framers of TAIKO were never able to clarify what was meant by "limited, small-scale military action" and, in any event, did not desire to do so because of their efforts to gain public understanding and consensus on defense policy. Thus TAIKO was left without any strategic concept. Furthermore since 1976, Japan's economic power has grown until it is next to that of the United States. Japan should therefore assume more responsibility for her own defense. Military muscle should be used to backup Japan's diplomatic efforts, especially to regain the Northern Islands seized by the Soviets in 1945. Diplomatic negotiations should, of course, be emphasized in seeking their return. Rather than considering how her military forces should be used in wartime, Japan should concentrate on how the Self Defense Forces can protect the national interest in peacetime. This approach would make weapon procurement policy more effective and realistic. It is essential to integrate Japan's defense policy with that of the United States, taking into account the international strategic interests of both countries. TAIKO, lacking in such conceptual and strategic guidance, is useless as a guidepost for protecting the present security interests of Japan.

Iwashima thought that as long as Mr. Sakata, the present Speaker of the

Lower House of the Diet, and a founding father of TAIKO was alive, little could be done to change TAIKO. To do so would cause Sakata to lose face. Also little change has occurred in Japan's political factional strife to permit serious consideration of modifications in TAIKO. Until a shift in public mood takes place, politicians will be reluctant to do anything about TAIKO.

CHUGYO

Comments about CHUGYO were relatively brief and were generally made in conjunction with remarks about TAIKO. Iwashima felt that if the new 5-year plan is successful, TAIKO might not be the obstacle to the defense effort that it is today. Most American officials hope for success of the new 5-year plan to achieve a level of defense capability that will allow Japan to assume more of the burden for her own defense.. They are pleased, Iwashima thought, that Mr. Nakasone was able to get the new plan to a national policy level.

Ito thought it illogical to have two defense plans, TAIKO and the new 5-year plan, as national defense policy. Under such circumstances, he believed it more reasonable to dispense with TAIKO and keep the new plan. He noted that while the new plan might cause defense spending to exceed 1% of GNP, it was reasonable to expect that it would not go much above 1% in deference to public opinion. He also observed that the new 5-year plan incorporates most of the principal elements of the former 1986-1990 CHUGYO.

Natsume said that the new 5-year plan was developed within the constraints established by TAIKO and if TAIKO were abrogated, the new plan would have to be expanded. Like TAIKO, the new plan does not include a conceptual framework to give guidance to defense planners. This is a serious weakness.

Nishihara thought that when the new 5-year plan is completed in 1990, questions about its relevance to building an effective Self Defense Force will likely be raised by those who oppose the defense buildup. One can argue, said Nishihara, that when the new 5-year plan is completed, TAIKO will no longer be necessary. But if TAIKO is abolished, it is probable that voices will be raised for a new TAIKO. In any event, Nishihara thought that in the interests of better U.S.-Japan security relations and in consideration of the growing Soviet threat and the need for a new strategic plan to counter the threat, it might be in Japan's best interests to revoke TAIKO in 1990.

Kitamura remarked that if the new 5-year plan proves successful, TAIKO should be abolished.

Several participants told me privately that the new plan was merely another name for CHUGYO and that it was conceived as a way that might lead to the ultimate elimination of the 1% policy and possibly the disappearance of TAIKO.

Session III

Summary and Recommendations

The principal thrust of the Kamata/Holland recommendations was for closer consultation on defense between Japan and the United States at various bureaucratic levels and between groups and institutions in the private sector.More effective collaboration, the paper contended,would bring better understanding and greater tolerance for the problems facing both nations as they sought to improve their respective security systems to meet the growing Soviet military threat in Northeast Asia.

While all participants endorsed in principle the major recommendations of the paper, they differed on questions of emphasis and approach. Nishihara believed that undue pressure on Japan would be counter-productive. While such pressure in the past has been advantageous to defense officials and some politicians in the Liberal Democratic Party who desire to see Japan's defense capability strengthened, over the long term, such continued pressure would hinder Japan's efforts to develop a sound defense policy. One practical approach for U.S.-Japan defense collaboration, in Nishihara's view, would be for the United States to give greater attention to building up the defense structure in the Hokkaido area. This would serve as a deterrent to Soviet political and military designs in the region. Nishihara emphasized the point made earlier by another participant that the Ministry of International Trade and Industry plays a relatively insignificant role in Japanese defense policy so should not be included in stepped-up consultations between officials of the two governments. On the other hand, he strongly endorsed the idea of educating the media to the realities of the threat and of Japans's defense responsibilities.

Yoshida believed that the United States should help the Japanese Government in every way possible to educate the Japanese people regarding the realities of the international situation in the Western Pacific. Japan must do her share in the defense of her homeland and continue to work closely with the United States to maintain security and peace in the area. The United States should especially help Japan to quiet the worries of ASEAN countries about Japanese rearmament.

Natsume contended that U.S.-Japan security relations were very satisfactory. The United States has been sensitive to Japan's problems in building up her defenses. Natsume thought that quiet dialogue was more preferable to heavy-handed diplomacy and would accomplish much more given the personality of the Japanese people. While there has been excellent service-to-service cooperation between the two countries, it is necessary to broaden the area of consultation to include policy-makers and legislators. By expanding the area of discussion, Japan can better anticipate the swings in American policy and make the necessary adjustments. It is important, said Natsume, that the United States maintain a steady policy course so that Japan-United States joint policy deliberations could be enhanced. Frictions over trade relations should be kept separate from the defense debate in order to avoid policy confusion and misunderstanding.

Onishi felt a serious problem facing the two nations was the difference in the perception of the threat. While Americans are deeply concerned over the

121

Soviet threat, the Japanese are less troubled by it. It is important that the two countries discuss their differences carefully to come to some common understanding over the degree of the Soviet menace and what both can do to deal with it. It is necessary for the Japanese to have a better understanding of U.S. policymaking, of the laws and regulations that affect U.S. ability to militarily carryout its commitments to its allies, of the mechanics of developing a defense budget and the priorities established for that purpose, and the roles of the Congress, the Executive Branch, special interest groups and the media in developing security policy. Such knowledge will help Japan to better understand the reliability of the American commitment to defend Japan under the U.S.-Japan Security Treaty. There are growing doubts in Japan about America's resolve to defend Japan and in order to curb such doubts, greater appreciation of the mechanics of the American policy-making system is necessary.

Kato also endorsed quiet diplomacy as the best way to promote mutual understanding. Japan cannot always comply with U.S. requests due to domestic political considerations and America must understand the reasons why. Style in negotiation is important and both countries should have a better appreciation of its relevance to the negotiating process.

Takubo said that both sides must understand the other's way of thinking on security matters. Japan's role in the defense process is influenced by domestic factors as well as conditions in the international environment. Takubo also pointed to the obvious when he said that Japan's parliamentary system produces different forces and influences in the way policy is made, contrasting the Japanese "way" with that of the U.S. presidential form of government. The Japanese system is decentralized and authority defused. The Prime Minister does not have the power of an American president. Unless the United States understands these differences, policy cooperation will become more and more difficult. The Japanese media, especially the Asahi, Mainichi, and the Tokyo Shimbun have distorted defense policy and have led the public to believe that any buildup of Japan's defense forces is another step back to militarism. The United States should try to influence the Japanese media to take a more realistic view of security. If this can be done, defense cooperation between the two countries will be strengthened.

Kitamura backed Takubo's views on the Japanese media and its impact on the Japanese public's thinking about defense. If the media could be persuaded to take a more realistic position on Japan's defense, the public would respond more favorably to the defense buildup and politicians and bureaucrats would be more willing to take forthright positions on security questions. This would help build closer defense cooperation between the two countries. The United States should be clear about the role it expects Japan to take in the mutual security partnership. Diet members and U.S. Congressmen could be very useful in moving the two countries closer to a clear understanding of each other's role in the defense system in Northeast Asia. While there has been effective cooperation at the service and bureaucratic levels, greater efforts need to be made to bring legislators into the defense process.

Iwashima contended that while there may be some limitation to what bureaucrats and legislators from both countries can discuss with each other, there is less prohibition in the academic area. Advantage should therefore be taken of existing private institutions to provide more clarity on difficult issues of defense.

Nishihara added the point that by promoting greater communication between the legislators of both countries, the entire spectrum of defense relations will improve. To give the impression that Japan is building her defenses to satisfy the United States is to confuse the issue. The Japanese Government should disabuse the public on this point.

Kato opined that it would be difficult to discuss the state of U.S.-Japan defense relations 10 years hence as conditions change. Policies that are based on such projections may not have relevance for realistic defense policymaking. In joint discussions on security policy, the Japanese and U.S. sides should be equal. At the present time in the Security Consultative Committee (SCC), Japan is represented by the Foreign Minister and the Director General of the Defense Agency whereas the American side is composed of the U.S. Ambassador to Japan and the Commander-in-Chief of Pacific Forces (CINCPAC). It would be better if the protocol level were even.

The United States must understand the important influences that are at work within the ruling Liberal Democratic Party. The yoto is broad enough in its philosophy to include the viewpoints of what Americans might consider to be the disparate views of Republicans and Democrats in American politics. Kato said there are sharp differences in the political postures of the yoto and yato. To understand this is to have a better grasp of the forces that influence security policy in Japan.

Ito said that the base point for mutual discussions on defense is for the American side to have a better grasp of the history of security policy in Japan; of the influence of the Constitution, of the preoccupation with the elimination of militarism after the war, of the amae feeling that Japanese have toward relations with the United States, and of a growing sense of Japan's economic power in the world. To develop the necessary consensus in Japan on defense policy can only be achieved by relating present day conditions to the past history of Japanese security. Mutual discussions as recommended in the Kamata/Holland report should be conducted on the basis of history as well as the reality of today.

Iwashima concluded the discussion by stating that in order to improve communication between the United States and Japan it is as important to have better understanding about Japanese defense among the Japanese as it is to have good communication between the two countries. It is incumbent on those in authority in Japan to educate the Japanese people on the full list of Japanese security problems so they can better understand the true nature of U.S.-Japan defense relations and why those relations are important for Japan's safety.

Participants

Aka, Raymond, American Embassy, Tokyo
Ito, Keiichi, Advisor, Mitsubishi Electric Corporation and former official
of the Defense Agency
Iwashima, Hisao, Professor, National Institute for Defense Studies
Kato, Ryozo, Foreign Ministry
Kitamura, Kenichi, Retired Admiral, Maritime Self Defense Forces
Masuzoe, Yoichi, Professor, Tokyo University
Nagano, Shigeto, Retired General, Ground Self Defense Forces
Natsume, Haruo, former Vice Minister, Defense Agency
Nishihara, Masashi, Professor, National Defense Academy
Onishi, Seiichiro, Executive Director, Research Institute for Peace and
Security
Sakanaka, Tomohisa, Professor, Aoyama Gakuin University; former reporter
for the Asahi Shimbun
Takubo, Tadae, Professor, Kyorin University; formerly with the JiJi Press
Yoshida, Manabu, Retired Admiral, Maritime Self Defense Forces

Associate Coordinator
   Kamata, Shin'ichi, Professor, National Defense Academy

Staff Assistant
   Kushizaki, Kumie

Notes

Chapter 1
1. General MacArthur's letter to Prime Minister Yoshida Shigeru, dated July 8, 1950. Courtesy of the Anmerican Embassy, Tokyo.
2. Liberal Star (Organ of the Liberal Democratic Party) March 10, 1986

Chapter 2
1. New York Times Magazine, September 7, 1986, Section 6.
2. Ibid
3. Testimony of Professor Gerald Curtis at hearings before the Committee on Foreign Affairs and its Subcommittee on International Economic Policy and Trade and Asian Pacific Affairs, 97th Congress, Second Session, March 17, 1982., p.388.
4. See John K. Emmerson's Arms, Yen, and Power: The Japanese Dilemma, Dunellen, 1973, p. 125

Chapter 5
1. For a discussion of the Sea Dragon issue, see Harrison Holland, Managing Diplomacy: The United States and Japan, Hoover Institution Press, 1984, pp. 128-130.

Chapter 6

1. Okazaki Hisahiko, The Political Framework of Japan's Defense - Defense Policies of Nations, Editors Murray and Viotti, Johns Hopkins University Press, 1983, pp. 468-473.

Chapter 8
1. Testimony of Professor Nathaniel Thayer at Hearings before the Committee on Foreign Affairs and its Subcommittee on International Economic Policy and Trade and Asian and Pacific Affairs, 97th Congress, Second Session, March 17, 1982., p.224.
2. Testimony of Professor Gerald Curtis before the Asian and Pacific Affairs Subcommittee of the 97th Congress, March 17, 1982., p.387.

Selected Bibliography

English

1. Government Decision-Making in Japan, Committee on Foreign Affairs, U.S. House of Representatives, 1982.
2. Hearings before SubCommittee on Asian and Pacific Affairs and on International Economic Policy and Trade, U.S. House of Representatives, June 1984.
3. Defense of Japan, 1984, Japan Defense Agency.
4. The United States and Japan: Problems in Perception, William Watts, September 1984.
5. United States-Japan Security Relations in the 1980s and Beyond, Ellen S. Frost, September 1984.
6. Defense Policies of Nations, Editors, Douglas Murray and Paul Viotti, Articles by John Endicott and Okazaki Hisahiko, Johns Hopkins University Press, 1983.
7. The United States-Japan Security Relationship in Transition, Institute for Foreign Policy Analysis and Japan Center for Study of Security Issues, August 1983.
8. The Military Balance in Northeast Asia: Challenge to Japan and Korea, Anthony Cordesman, Armed Forces Journal, December 1983.
9. East Asia: Another Year of Living Dangerously, Chalmers Johnson, Foreign Affairs, 1984.
10. The Pacific Naval Balance, Benjamin Schemmer, Armed Forces Journal, April 1984.
11. Defense Burden-Sharing: United States Relations with NATO allies and Japan, Stanley Sloan, Library of Congress, December 1982.
12. The Japan-United States Defense Relationship, Suzuki Yoshikatsu, Arms Control Seminar, Stanford University, 1983.
13. Japanese Security and the United States, Muraoka Kunio, International Institute of Strategic Studies, 1973.
14. United States-Japan Security Relations, Nishihara Masashi and Richard Betts, 6th Shimoda Conference, 1983.
15. A Military Buildup, Larry Niksch, Foreign Service Journal, March 1983.
16. Defending the New Japan, John Glenn, The Washington Quarterly, 1982.
17. American Embassy, Tokyo Translation Service, 1984/1985.
18 Japan Times, 1984/1985.
19 Defense Bulletin, Foreign Press Center, Tokyo, October 1981.
20. Japan Economic Survey, Vol. VIII, No. 4, April 1984.
21. Report on Comprehensive National Security, Comprehensive National Security Group, July 2,1980.
22. Japan's Defense Posture, Masagoe Yoichi, Pacific Basin Seminar, Hoover Institution, August 1983.
23. Alternative Futures in United States-Japan Relations, Pepper, Janow amd Wheeler: Long Term Scenarios in Japan-United States Relations, Tanaka Akihiko, University of Tokyo, United States-Japan Advisory Commission, September 1984.
24. New York Times, 1984/1985.

25.Defense of Sea Lanes, Asian Security, Research Institute for Peace and Security, Tokyo, 1983.
26.Congressional Record, Senate, S. 15833, December 20,1982.
27.International Security, Vol. 8, No. 3, Winter, 1983/4.

Japanese

1. Soshiki to Kikan in Boei Nenkan, 1981. (Defense Almanac).
2. Heiwaji no boeiryoku, Kobo Takuya, April 1973, pp. 12-26.
3. Boei Antena (February & September 1984).
4. Definition of Defense Budget.
5. Ratio of defense budget to other spending.
6. United States-Japan Security System from International Point of View, Kato Ryozo, Japanese Ministry of Foreign Affairs, May 20,1983.
7. Problems Concerning the Foundations of the Japanese Defense Structure; Relations between politics and the military, Research Institute for Peace and Security, June 1983.
8. Strategic Argument and American Public Opinion. A discussion by Okazaki Hisahiko, Japanese Foreign Ministry and Shiina Motoo, LDP member of the Lower House of the Diet, Shokun, New York edition, 1985.
9. Discussion of the 1% ceiling on the defense budget by Okazaki Hisahiko and Shiina, Motoo, Shokun, February 1985.
10.Discussion of the 1% ceiling on the defense budget by Ito Keiichi, Chuo Koran, March 1985.
11.The International Situation and Japanese Defense, Kaihara Osamu, Speech at the Industrial Club, Tokyo, No. 806.
12.How Secure is the Ocean Supply Route?, Kaihara Osamu, Sekai Shuho, February 2, 1981.
13.Ask Prime Minister Nakasone about 3 points - How can one understand politics?, *Sankei Shimbun*, January 25, 1985.
14. Chuki Gyomu Mitsumori (56 CHUGYO).

Abbreviations

ASDF - Air Self Defense Forces
GNP   - Gross National Product
GSDF - Ground Self Defense Forces
JDA   - Japan Defense Agency
LDP   - Liberal Democratic Party
MSDF - Maritime Self Defense Forces
MITI - Ministry of International Trade and Industry
NDC   - National Defense Council
PARC - Policy Affairs Research Council
SDF   - Self Defense Forces
SDI   - Strategic Defense Initiative

Index